Grading with a Purple Crayon

A Developmental Approach to High School Composition for Homeschooling Families

Dena M. Luchsinger

CRECER PUBLICATIONS
WASILLA, ALASKA

Requests for permission should be addressed to:

Crecer Publications
1161 N. Iroquois Drive
Wasilla, Alaska 99654

Includes bibliographical references and index.
ISBN 978-0-9848313-2-6 (paper)

Printed in the United States of America
First edition published 2012

To Gary:
You teach me what it means to persevere.

TABLE OF CONTENTS

Part 1: Basic Compositions, Essential Skills & Qualities

Part 2: Advanced Compositions for College-Bound Students

Part 1

Basic Compositions:

Essential Skills & Qualities

Chapter 1

The Purple Crayon Rationale

I never thought I would homeschool. Not only did I grow up attending public schools, I always assumed that the professionally trained teachers in public schools could do a better job teaching my children than I ever could. And, to a certain extent, I still believe that. The certified teachers in public schools certainly do better at teaching classes of twenty to thirty diverse students than I would. I'm terrible at multi-tasking.

But when my oldest daughter Kristen started struggling in middle school, it was clear that she needed a change. Her grades had fallen dramatically, and she was visibly miserable. When we asked what could be done for her at school, a guidance counselor told us that Kristen's teachers could give her a seat near the front of the class and remind her to turn in her homework.

"That's it?" I asked. My daughter had been diagnosed by an educational psychologist with situational depression—in other words, school was depressing her—and the offer on the table was *nagging*? It wasn't enough—in fact, it wasn't even close. So, while I hardly felt competent to teach her, my husband and I removed Kristen from public school mid-way through the school year. Much to my surprise, I discovered that I loved teaching her at home, so much so that we took her sister out of elementary school the following fall, and I have been having a wonderful time teaching our girls at home ever since.

The "It's Done When it Looks Like Something I Could Have Written Myself" Years

When we removed Kristen from public school, I was terrified I would only make matters worse. She was already suffering from an anxiety disorder, and she was coping with life by reading and re-reading the same books. I knew she was not going to learn much that way, but a big part of me wanted to take pressure off of her, especially those first few months. At the same time, I worried that Kristen was not going to learn anything at home. I decided to compromise by postponing a few of the more stressful subjects and using Kristen's fascination—some might say, obsession—with wild cats to motivate her to practice writing.

That semester, she wrote "Cheetahs: Big Cat or Savannah Dog?", "Lions, Tigers, and Jaguars, Oh My!", her favorite essay, "Something's Eating Me . . . Is it a Leopard or a Cheetah?", and "Lion King Lies!" a passionate clarification of factual inaccuracies about lions in her favorite Disney movie. Oh, yeah; she was a little obsessed.

The problem was that Kristen's essays, while not terrible, never quite met my standards. I wasn't sure what to do about that. When I started teaching Kristen at home, I'd assumed that writing would be the one subject I knew how to teach. I was rusty in algebra, and science was never my forte, but I thought that since I was a writer myself, I had it under control. But whereas math, science, social studies—basically, every other subject—came with answer keys, writing seemed hopelessly subjective. Admittedly, my standards were pretty high—perhaps unreasonably so—but my grading plan was actually simple: any essay that seemed as if I had written it myself was good. Anything else was, well . . . not.

So I would sit down at the computer and show Kristen how to fix her papers, moving paragraphs up or down, combining sentences, adjusting her word choices, and generally tweaking the whole thing. Though I sometimes wondered if I wasn't taking over a little too much, I didn't have any better ideas, so I kept doing what seemed to be working in spite of my doubts. Once I even asked one of my daughter's friends how her mother graded her writing. Their family had been homeschooling longer than we had, and I knew my friend was very good at it. I was amused and relieved when her daughter answered, "Oh, she just assigns me an essay and I write it; then she tells me what's wrong with it, and I revise it about ten times until it looks like something she might have written herself."

My process precisely! I felt comforted.

Still, I wasn't entirely appeased, so when another friend recommended an online tutoring service, I decided to give it a try. Since I was busy working on a master's degree in writing myself and responding to Kristen's essays was the most time-consuming of all of my homeschool-related chores, it sounded like just the thing. Unfortunately, Kristen's tutor taught no better than I had, and maybe worse. Her e-mails all began and ended with sugary praise, but the gist of her instruction was basically that Kristen should stop making spelling mistakes and do a better job of "hooking" her. Kristen didn't like her, her writing saw no improvement, and at the end of the semester, we were both glad to be rid of her.

Then our advisor recommended an online program that assigned essays a holistic score. We gave it a try, but it too seemed to focus on identifying technical errors. Out of curiosity, I tried entering a few of my own essays into the computer and discovered that it couldn't tell much about the quality of the essays I'd entered: the program had no sense of rhythm or humor, no awareness of precision, concision, or coherence. It was like a computerized version of the tutor, without the sugary praise, which, strangely enough, was actually something of an improvement.

The Big Guessing Game

The problem with teaching composition is that there is no answer key like there is for math or science. With writing, there are a million ways to answer any given writing prompt. How do you grade that? Well, if you're like most teachers, you start marking the stuff you know is wrong: "That's spelled wrong, you forgot to capitalize Louisiana, that's a fragment, you didn't indent." So far so good. Next is the tricky part, but you plow on: "This is vague, that's kind of awkward, this part's confusing, and that just plain doesn't sound good. Plus, I don't like your introduction." Lacking any other starting place for grading, most teachers adopt what I call the 'red pen approach': you see a mistake, you know it's wrong, you flag it: "Look here: see this? That's wrong. Fix it."

What're students supposed to do with all of that feedback? Usually, so much negative feedback frustrates students and flusters them, and while they might go back and write it over again, often as not, they're just complying with orders and guessing at what you want them to write. They might get a lot of practice writing, but without clear ideas about what constitutes good quality in a piece of writing, they tend to continually try new things rather than cementing any particular quality. Most frustrating of all, the rules seem to change from week to week: one week, it's "this point needs more development" and the next week, an earnest attempt at more development is "redundant" or "off topic." Writing feels like a big guessing game.

Part of the issue is the complexity of writing at the high school level. In elementary and middle school, writing skills are taught in isolation: students learn spelling, vocabulary, capitalization, punctuation, basic grammar, and sentence construction. Later, students learn how to organize basic paragraphs and simple compositions, usually with very simple themes and often with ready-made structures so that the exercise is little more strenuous than a fill-in-the-blank exercise. But by the time students enter high school, compositions are complex. Students are expected to balance all of the elements of strong writing: organization, conventions, content, word choice, fluency, voice, and style, and on top of all that, they are to do so with any of a dozen types of compositions. It's like going from trying to toss and catch a single ball to juggling five or six. For some crazy reason, when it comes to teaching composition, instead of tossing students one more ball to work in at a time, we pelt 'em with all six at once—and then we wonder why they drop some of them.

Waves of Insight

Gradually, I began to see little ways I could improve the way I taught writing to my daughter. Uncomfortable with my overbearing "coaching" and the red pen approach that felt critical even to me, I started to look for a better way. In time, I pieced together a revised program based on insights I slowly gained as a writer, as a writing student, as a tutor, and as a teacher of writing.

The first wave of insight came when I went back to school for a master's degree in writing. As a student of writing, I learned from my own teachers, and one of the more helpful things that my mentors did was tell me what I was doing right. Whereas I'd had professors praise my papers at times in the past, the mentors in my writing program were specific when they told me what they liked about my writing, so I knew which of my instincts were on and which were off. Knowing that expletive constructions were weak and parallel structures were strong taught me so much more than vague comments like "awkward" and "nice!" in the margins of my papers. The more I understood about writing, the more responsible I could be for my own improvement, and the more confident I felt as a writer.

After finishing my master's program, I began tutoring writing students, first within our homeschooling community, and later at a local community college. Tutoring professionally taught me that it is one thing to edit someone else's writing so that it reads like you think it should and quite another to show students how they can write well enough to get their own ideas across clearly. Working with both adults taking remedial writing classes and high school students, I have been able to observe what issues crop up most often, and I have enjoyed designing little mini-lessons to help my students understand problematic patterns and revise them in their own writing.

Still more insights came during my brief excursion into the field of education. After a few positive experiences tutoring high school students within our local homeschooling community, a few parents encouraged me to consider teaching secondary English. Encouraged, I enrolled in a graduate education program. I ultimately decided that teaching in the public education system was not for me, but I found my courses and a few of my texts—especially Ralph Tyler's ideas about designing instruction—really helpful. I became convinced that setting clear goals first and then preparing opportunities for students to practice them facilitates progress far more than assigning writing projects willy nilly. I also came across a way to use rubrics as a functional tool for teaching students, not just for testing them. It was just the approach I'd been looking for.

Basically, the approach is simple: It involves limiting the number of objectives for evaluating essays and retaining the same format and basic purposes for writing tasks over a fairly long period of time. By isolating the skills that are being graded, students can focus and teachers can measure progress more easily. By identifying six of the most important goals for students at the beginning of the period, reviewing how to resolve persistent issues in any piece of writing, and offering students multiple opportunities to practice, students not only make discernable progress on a reasonable number of objectives, but grading becomes entirely transparent. Students can grade their own essays if they like, or at least understand how you came up with the grade you did.

From Red Pen to Purple Crayon

Of course, it is one thing to theorize and quite another to implement a program, so I was eager to try using a rubric as a teaching tool for improving the overall quality of my daughter's writing. Kristen's senior year, she and one of her friends agreed to study U.S. Government by reading and writing about the Constitution, the Federalist and Anti-Federalist papers, and the Bill of Rights. Their first assignment was to compare and contrast the Constitution with the Articles of Confederation. Those first papers served as a benchmark, and we used them to determine appropriate goals for improving each girl's writing over the rest of the semester. These goals were identified clearly and objectively in a rubric which targeted six specific objectives.

Over the subsequent twelve weeks, we all wrote a number of response essays, and we used the rubric we'd devised to evaluate each paper—our own and each others'. I believe we used crayons for this. Since the criteria were objective, the girls learned to be critical of their own efforts. Soon, they were making necessary revisions before submitting their essays, and their scores improved. By the end of the semester, both girls had virtually eradicated all six of their former weaknesses, and the quality of their writing had improved to the point that both girls were easily writing as well as a typical college freshman.

How This Book is Different

So many composition programs claim to teach educators how to teach writing, you might wonder how this one differs. Here are a few ways that this program is different from other high school composition courses:

Other composition courses	This course . . . .
Expect students to write correctly, with the quality of polished writers, and they grade them down if they don't	Expects students to develop greater quality and eradicate writing tics over time; grades reflect specific, identifiable objectives
Employ ambiguous and subjective rubrics (i.e., "excellent" versus "very good" word choices) as tools for grading	Uses clear and objective rubrics (i.e., "sentences do not employ the expletive construction") as tool for both teaching and evaluating student writing
Pretend that students write for many diverse audiences and purposes when, in fact, they submit everything to a teacher	Acknowledges that students write for an academic audience and purpose
Consider creative writing essential to the basic course	Considers creative writing inessential; advises students who enjoy writing for purposes of expression or entertainment to pursue these through other electives

Some people may disagree with some aspects of this program, and I don't deny that in many ways, this program is a departure from what is standard in many courses. And yet, I've met with many parents following other composition programs who are confused by supposedly enticing creative writing exercises that neither entice their students nor lead them to mastery and frustrated by programs that call for perfection but never seem to move students in that direction. This program, on the other hand, assures slow but steady progress. Of course, a percentage of students seem to have a knack for writing and don't seem to need any particular program at all, but these are by far the minority. Realistically, most students need structure and consistent practice to learn how to write. That's what this program prescribes.

In this book, I'm going to suggest that composition skills should be taught in a logical order. As with math, students continue to practice skills until they demonstrate mastery. Only then do students continue on to the next layer of skills. I'm also going to argue that grades should reflect *only* the skill set in question, not the quality of the composition as a whole. Students should be rewarded for working hard and acquiring new skills, and not be continually punished for not having mastered all of the skills and qualities expected of professional writers. By using a tailored rubric each semester, scores reflect improvement, not a subjective judgment call. Students feel secure in their writing ability, and the guessing game goes away. Finally, I am going to recommend that composition prompts derive from all subjects, not just topics typical of language arts. By applying composition skills across academic subjects, students get more practice writing and make the most efficient use of their time.

I'd also like to help you see the task of scoring essays as one that is manageable. When objectives are clear and objective, you never need to criticize because students can see as well as you how their efforts align with standards. Teaching composition is much more user and teacher friendly when you break it down into the pieces that make it up. The best part of this analytic, developmental approach to teaching and grading compositions is that you can toss out your red pens and critical comments. Instead, you can be the second set of eyes that helps students find their own growing edges and the voice of encouragement that helps them grow. Buy a box of Crayolas, divvy them up between you and your student, and see if you don't agree that it's a lot more friendly and effective to do your grading with a purple crayon.

Chapter 2

Logical Progression

I bought my youngest daughter's second grade math curriculum because it had gotten good reviews, and also, because it was bright and cheerful. I don't remember why it had gotten good reviews, but I soon decided that the cheeriness was about the only thing going for it—and even that began to annoy us after a while. You see, the topics kept skipping around. Every chapter, it was something new. If one chapter taught double-digit addition, the next one would be graphs. After graphs, we'd learn basic multiplication. Then telling time, then fractions, then money. I think there were eight topics per quarter, and only after you'd covered them all would you learn the next gradation of difficulty for each topic, which by then you hadn't seen for two months so you'd have to re-learn it before you could move on. It seemed a pretty inefficient way to do math.

I suspect the curriculum was designed by someone who wanted to make sure kids had covered all of the grade-level content standards by state testing time in April. Which is a great way to slow down learning, if you think about it. But! The pictures were sure bright and cheerful.

A lot of secondary writing programs and curriculums do exactly the same thing. They skip around and switch up tasks continually. One week it's narratives, next week it's exposition. In high school, freshmen are often expected to compose business letters, short stories, autobiographical narratives, literary analyses, and persuasive, research, and analytical essays—even though most of these require students to learn different formats, skills, and tones. So distinct are the various writing discourses, students never have a chance to cement their understanding of any one of them, much less get a hold on any particular quality of writing. Instead, they necessarily focus their mental energies on adhering to the various rules that correspond to each writing task's peculiarities, whether that is the form of a business letter, finding their personal voice in a creative writing application, or weaving a colorful narrative together with real academic content. Constantly switching up writing assignments might keep writing class interesting, but it exposes students to peculiarities of writing at the expense of effectively teaching and reinforcing the basics.

Eventually, I gave up on the bright and cheery second grade math program and ordered something called "Developmental Math." That curriculum was not bright nor was it cheery—in fact, it was monochromatic and practically devoid of illustrations—but it worked. Each book focused on a single aspect of math and broke it down into the segments that would make the concepts attainable to young students. The books were ordered to teach basic operations first and then incorporated these operations into the more challenging problems that came later. All math programs do this to a certain extent, but this one purposefully eliminated peripheral topics so that nothing interrupted the logical order of lessons. Rather than jumping around and necessitating re-teaching for previously covered topics, each lesson reinforced the previous one and facilitated mastery.

There's no reason why high school composition can't work the same way. Rather than continually interrupting the logical sequence of basic writing skills with peripheral ones, the composition course itself focuses on acquiring basic writing skills and qualities in an order that facilitates students' building on success. Skills such as citing sources and hooking readers are held off until students are ready for them, while still other inessential skills are omitted entirely or treated as electives.

Prioritizing Essential Writing Skills, Postponing Peripheral Ones

Most state content standards assert that students need to write for a variety of purposes and should, therefore, practice many diverse types of writing tasks annually. Rather than honing basic skills, most high school students practice writing stories and poems and letters and multimedia presentations and persuasive essays and literary analyses every year. Yes, basic skills are expected of students at all times, but students quite often fall short of those expectations because they are trying to simultaneously learn conventions, formatting, and tones that are particular to these diverse assignments. Such an approach forces students to shift gears on a regular basis, making it difficult to master or even identify what is basic.

A beginning writer is a lot like a beginning ice skater. If you have ever watched accomplished ice skaters practice, you will have noticed that even highly skilled skaters take time to warm up with basic skills like crossovers before going on to practice jumps. Novices, meanwhile, do little but work on perfecting posture, strokes, and crossovers. No doubt they'd love to skip the boring stuff and just do stunts, but skaters learn very quickly that when they skip the basics, they wind up on their butts. And it takes a lot of practice to master those basics.

So it is with composition. If you want a student to really write well, you have to spend a lot of time working on the basics: clear content, essential conventions, overall coherence. After getting these solidly down, students practice these same skills with more challenging applications. Finally, students learn the more advanced skills of writing eloquent paragraphs and citing authoritative sources. By affording students many practice attempts to fortify strategies for achieving certain qualities in their writing, students hone and gradually improve their abilities.

I am convinced that part of the reason so many students graduate from high school without achieving the ability to communicate clearly in writing is that educators fail to prioritize clarity as the single quality that grounds all good writing. Oddly—insanely, perhaps—it seems that most language arts programs challenge students from primary school on to revise their writing not for clarity but for style, switching up basic and boring words and adding details so that their final draft is more striking, colorful, elegant, or fresh.

In fact, adding details where none are called for makes sense only when you're writing primarily to entertain. But is the ability to entertain other people by writing the skill that secondary students need to get by in the world? Most of the writing that adults do for any functional purpose in the real world—such as pursuing a college degree or conducting business or arguing for fair treatment by government bureaucracy—is better off written plainly: with a neutral voice, specific, accurate words, and clear, well-ordered sentences. Ayn Rand (2001) puts it this way:

> Writing is literally only the skill of putting down on paper a clear thought, in clear terms. Everything else, such as drama and 'jazziness,' is merely the trimmings. I once said that the three most important elements of fiction are plot, plot, and plot. The equivalent in nonfiction is clarity, clarity, and clarity. (p. 2)

Clear prose immediately impresses people that the writer is an intelligent individual worth hearing. People who can't convey their concerns clearly in writing are often disrespected and disregarded by those in authority, putting them at a huge disadvantage in the world. Think about it: the ability to have your concerns taken seriously by large and small businesses, health insurance companies, school districts, and government bureaucracies largely hinges on the ability to communicate clearly. And don't think that writing is just one form of communication, because although it is just one, it is a biggie. Not only do letters provide a record of communication that bureaucracies have to take seriously, but people who write clearly usually speak more coherently, too.

Writing to convey ideas clearly and coherently is essential; this is where students should get the bulk of their writing practice. Sure, it might be fun to compose a witty essay, meaningful to express a hard-to-express idea in a beautiful poem, or lofty to take a crack at a narrative that conveys a truthful theme—but remember that the authors who do these things well are specialists. Essayists, novelists, humorists, and poets, if they are successful—that is, if they write so well that other people are willing to pay to read their work—tend to possess exceptional giftedness and an insatiable desire to write well, and they generally nurture this skill and practice it for years. Meanwhile, students who compose an occasional expressive piece of writing because it has been assigned can only be said to be dabbling. Needless to say, dabblers rarely become skilled.

In fact, the ability to write for expressive purposes well is highly unlikely in adolescents: W. H. Auden argues that a promising young writer is revealed neither by originality nor by powerful emoting on paper, but by demonstrating technical skill with language (as cited in Gardner, p. 82). Note that expressive writing is not the way to teach writing skills of either the functional or expressive sort: it is specifically the technical ability to convey content clearly that develops them both.

A developmentally appropriate composition program does not ask students to perform triple axles. Not only do I exclude most expressive and imaginative purposes from this course, I don't believe students new to composition writing have any business attempting involved literary analyses or research projects. Most freshmen haven't mastered basic writing conventions. They shouldn't be focusing their efforts on quoting texts or citing sources. That's a peripheral skill—and by peripheral, I mean that these abilities don't apply to every writing application, only some. Clarity and content must come first. To require students to quote and cite sources before they have mastered conveying content clearly is like asking a skater to learn back crossovers while juggling scarves: only the most weirdly talented is going to manage it with any degree of success. Postpone advanced academic compositions until students have mastered writing with clarity and coherence, and when they're ready, students will quickly incorporate those new challenges with ease.

Mastery, Not Variety; Authenticity, Not Pretense

Students resent being asked to constantly perform without ever being allowed to perfect their writing skills. Most writing programs set students up to continually fall short and then wonder why students don't like it. I know why: constant criticism hurts. It hurts a student's dignity to put forth his or her best effort and continually be told it's not good enough. And yet, instead of repeating the tasks and coaching students so that they might improve, most programs force students to take new risks with new forms, which, not surprisingly, students fail to master as well.

It is a mistake to credit this resentment to being asked to write, period. Many educators mistakenly imagine that what students lack is motivation or ownership, not a clear and reasonable developmental process. So what do they do? They offer students more "ownership" and "personal choice" by making students do creative writing, some of which educators now like to call "authentic" writing tasks. According to experts Grant Wiggins and Jay McTighe (2005), authentic tasks "simulate or replicate important real-world challenges" (p. 337). An example of an "authentic" writing prompt might be: "Imagine you are the newly selected poet laureate of the European Union and have been commissioned to write a sonnet about events in the Middle East. It will be published in the *Jerusalem Times* as well as in the *Cairo Daily News*. Your goal is to promote empathy for the people suffering on both sides of this struggle" (Wiggins & McTighe, p. 166).

Most of the high school students I know understand that when you pretend to be someone you are not, you're not being "authentic," you're pretending—which means "fake." For the most part, the only authentic creative writing I have seen among adolescents comes from students who independently get an idea and want to pursue it on their own, voluntarily writing unsolicited essays, editorials, poems, stories, fan-fictions, and even novels, often with the intent to publish their work. Students who write for genuinely authentic purposes do so autonomously and almost never for the sake of a grade. To be clear: there is only one authentic purpose for a high school composition course: to help students develop strong writing skills. Trying to motivate students by pretending something is "authentic" when it is not insults their intelligence.

Students might resent teachers treating them as if they're foolish and wasting their time, but I don't believe students resent learning to write. People generally yearn to develop; they inherently crave improvement. Some of the adults I've met as a community college tutor tell me how much they delight in finally learning to read and write after years of getting by without being able to read so much as a fast food menu. Learning was hard for them, but gratifying; what they resented in school wasn't learning itself, but being ineffectively taught and then berated and blamed for their failure.

Efficient Applications

Homeschooling educators have an advantage when it comes to assigning writing prompts: they can double-dip. Compositions don't all have to be about topics related to English—in fact, I would suggest that at least two-thirds of the content for compositions should come from other subject areas: social studies, science, health—whatever your student is studying. Writing regularly doesn't have to increase students' workload.

As with any skill, perfection comes through regular practice. People who wish to acquire skills understand that they must deliberately dedicate time or real skill will never develop. How well do you want to play a musical instrument, sculpt, dance, woodwork, run, ski, or skate? Whatever level of skill you hope to accomplish, you practice accordingly. If you want your high school student to write competently, he or she will need to spend at least two or three hours and preferably four or five hours writing paragraphs and essays weekly.

That much time might disgruntle students who feel they are wasting their time. And in all fairness, writing prompts like "What is your favorite hobby?" do just that. Such prompts do not address issues that students wish or need to explore. But high school students have a lot of legitimate work to do, classifying information and understanding difficult concepts from courses such as history, literature, economics, science, and health. Let students apply their composition efforts to this work. This allows students to simultaneously organize and cement knowledge while getting meaningful writing practice.

Students should never be required to make up silly stuff just to practice writing skills when they have plenty of real work to do already. Writing paragraphs or essays instead of completing the pre-fabricated true-false, multiple-choice, and fill-in-the-blank type worksheets that come with so many curriculums not only documents learning, but also provides valuable writing practice that students need. Writing also challenges students to organize and restate information, facilitating understanding and cementing knowledge. When students understand that writing can replace what they see as busy work and tests that require them to cram but rarely help them remember anything long-term, they realize that writing gives them double the value for their time and effort.

Basic and Advanced Levels

Just as a solid math program first teaches addition and subtraction, then multiplication and division, and finally factions and decimals, an efficient composition course helps students develop basic skills in a logical order. Using the five-paragraph form for initial efforts, students first summarize and classify information. The emphasis at this point in the program is in helping students learn how to convey content clearly and correctly as well as to gain practice with generalizations and abstraction. Next, students add the abilities to explain and then persuade. At this level, students must demonstrate reason and write with coherence, since any attempt at explanation or persuasion that is unreasonable or incoherent necessarily fails. The ability to analyze and discern subtle similarities and distinctions between concepts and situations is the last item students master in the basic high school program. Students who demonstrate mastery in using the five-paragraph essay to inform, explain, persuade, and compare and contrast concepts progress to the advanced writing course, which includes analyzing and synthesizing research and incorporating quotations from sources responsibly and eloquently. Finally, an addendum targeting non-academic purposes provides guidance for students who wish to experiment with writing personal essays, editorials, and journal articles as well as advice for students applying for jobs or college.

So Where does Creative Writing Come in?

It doesn't. For this composition course, students don't have to do any creative writing unless they want to. Students who are forced to write imaginatively against their will tend to do so very poorly, while students who feel the need to write imaginatively almost always do so on their own. Such students love expressing themselves in writing and always will—they don't need teachers to assign it. Meanwhile, forcing high school students to dedicate time to imaginative writing deprives them of practice they need to attain the essential skills they will need to succeed in college, to secure jobs, and to survive in the real world.

Now, if your student enjoys writing stories, by all means, encourage your student to do so in his or her leisure time or as another elective course. Imaginative writing help students develop an appreciation for the nuances of language and certainly affords valuable practice. In fact, for this reason alone, you might accept a few imaginative pieces in lieu of academic essays; at the same time, however, the goals of expressive or imaginative writing are quite distinct from those of academic writing. Students cannot learn clarity nor coherence from writing stories. Nor, in fact, are students likely to develop their imaginative writing skills to the degree they would if they were to focus first on learning the essential technical abilities that all good writing demands. Therefore, at the high school level, I encourage you to prioritize what is essential and treat writing for personal expression or entertainment as electives or extra-curricular activities.

A Word about Spelling

Some high school students struggle with spelling in spite of years of spelling instruction. Often, students whose instincts continually steer them wrong are merely doing what they believe they have been instructed to do. I recently read an essay written by a student with poor spelling, and I had to think a minute before I understood that the word 'fuchur' in his paper meant 'future.' Clearly, he had used his knowledge of phonics to "sound out" the word, and just as clearly, sounding out 'future' didn't work. As educational psychologist Diane McGuinness (1997) points out, "phonics programs do not teach phoneme awareness, nor do they teach the correct logic for the alphabet code" (p. 310). Phonics programs teach kids to memorize an assortment of rules and then mention that there are like a bajillion exceptions to these so-called "rules"—so many, in fact, that many kids never feel certain about when the rules apply, and when they don't. Confused, these students tend to guess at how to spell words, and because they don't trust their own instincts, they often guess wrong. Unfortunately, the more they do, the more frustrated these students feel, and the more reluctant they are to try.

If this sounds like your student, I would encourage you: your student can be successful as a speller and as a writer. I would also offer you a few suggestions. First, don't give up on spelling or assume that a spell-checker is going to solve the problem. Spell-checkers can't tell when a student has written the wrong word, and many word processors will auto-correct words to the closest approximation based on the letters a student has typed, which sometimes results in grossly erroneous word choices.

Second, make a point of prioritizing phonemic awareness and teaching syllabication, potentially using a curriculum such as Educators Publishing Service's *Megawords* series by Kristin Johnson and Polly Bayrd. Students who don't hear the subtle sounds in words—which is at least half of the problem, especially with boys—and students who don't understand the logic behind the spelling of words that "break the rules"—like future—never feel like they can convey their thoughts clearly in writing. Worse yet, many of them lose confidence in their ideas, period. This is a tragic, especially since these students can be trained to hear the sounds they're missing, and they can learn the spelling alternatives that English words employ. Most phonics programs teach children neither.

Finally, don't mark spelling errors on essays until your student has shown improvement in his or her spelling overall. Students who struggle with spelling often feel defeated by continually getting low scores on essays. Therefore, overlook spelling errors, especially on first drafts, and focus on your student's other goals. For instance, if your student is working on developing paragraphs, when you go over drafts, ignore spelling when you critically consider how well paragraphs are developed. Only later, on the revised draft, write corrections above any misspelled words and have your student correct the errors for the final version: no pressure, but also, no tolerance. Misspelled words do prevent readers from understanding, and you do your student no favors by pretending they don't.

For those students who only occasionally misspell words, treat spelling errors as you would any other error: five or more errors per page on an essay gets a 'requires revision'.

How to Use This Book

This book is not meant to be read cover-to-cover; rather, the sections and chapters of this book describe the forms, purposes, qualities and skills that students will need as they need them. Unless you want a preview of what lies ahead, you don't have to read the entire book before implementing the program, just the first six chapters. After that, you will need to read on only when your student is ready for the next level of challenge. The table below demonstrates the order of purposes and skills taught in this course as well as the approximate timeframe in which a typical student might progress through them.

Approximate Timeframe	Writing Purpose	Emphasis on Quality
Freshman & Sophomore Years	Inform	Content
	Explain	Clarity
	Persuade	Coherence
	Compare and Contrast	Eloquence
Junior & Senior Years	Analyze	Correctness
	Synthesize	Citations
Addendum to Course (Use when appropriate)	Entertain or Other Real World Application	Connecting with an Audience

That, in a nutshell, is the high school composition course I propose. In the next chapter, I will outline for you the process by which you can individualize your student's program so that, wherever he or she is along the progression of writing tasks and abilities, you can tailor a program that will help your student to grow.

Chapter 3

Rubric Design

When Kristen entered high school, she agreed that writing short essays would be a better way to document her work in history than completing worksheets and taking tests, and she also agreed that she'd rather write about history than random topics. So I assigned prompts for essays which she would write and revise until I was satisfied that the essay was as good as it was going to be. What I couldn't figure out, though, was how to get beyond that mark—because Kristen's writing skills reached a certain level, and then they seemed to stall. And while the essays she wrote were okay, they never seemed to improve.

One of the things I did to help her improve the quality of her writing was print out a "Comprehensive 6-point Writing Rubric" I found online and tack it next to her computer. The rubric consisted of a thirty-six box grid that distinguished levels of quality in the categories of content, organization, voice, word choices, fluency and conventions. I reasoned that seeing this rubric would somehow help Kristen write essays that were excellent in every possible way.

Unfortunately, the rubric kept falling behind the computer where I'd have to fish it out, dust it off, put it back up where Kristen could see it. I'd remind Kristen it was there and she'd answer dutifully that she did, and I'd rest assured, knowing that Kristen could just look at it and understand that the clear difference between good and great word choices was that great word choices were not only "specific and accurate" but "striking" as well. So-so word choices, on the other hand, were "mostly correct" but potentially lacking in "color," while poor ones involved colorful language that was "overdone."

For the longest time, I couldn't see how Kristen could have that rubric sitting right next to her and not be writing her essays with consistently "striking" words and "gripping" introductions. Wasn't it clear that was the goal?

Then one day, as I pulled the rubric out of the dusty crevice behind the desk, I took a good look at it and finally realized why it wasn't helping. How is Kristen supposed to know whether I'm going to find her words "striking" versus "overdone?" I realized that even I didn't know exactly what those words meant, but one was an A and the other a D. Or how, for instance, was Kristen going to know whether her "manipulation of conventions" would be considered "stylistic" or problematic—another difference between an A and a D? It finally hit me that the rubric was vague and confusing, and even if the distinctions between categories had been clearer, the sheer number of objectives was unmanageable.

In all fairness, the rubric I'd printed was designed for assessors, not for students. Its purpose—and the purpose of all rubrics, really—is to help teachers grade more objectively. Yet the more I looked at the rubric, I realized that much of what I found on the rubric was either contradictory or unclear. Might not one teacher find "striking" what another finds "overdone?" Even the so-called experts disagree about such things. It seemed to me that a rubric that was meant to help teachers grade more objectively should eliminate criteria that permitted such subjective judgment calls. But when I looked for a rubric that I liked better, I discovered that many rubrics were just like the one I'd printed, or even more subjective, doing little more than breaking writing down into its various aspects and suggesting teachers rate each of these as "excellent", "good," "adequate," or "poor."

And yet, while the comprehensive rubric I'd found was negligibly useful, the idea of a rubric in general still intrigued me. It seemed to me that a rubric could be a useful tool for students as well as assessors—because ideally, students should be able to assess their own work in some way. I reasoned that if students understood what they were trying to accomplish, they would necessarily be more likely to achieve it. I felt certain that an objective grading device would help me get rid of my subjective and sometimes strident grading approach and simultaneously empower Kristen to identify and fix the flaws in her own writing.

RUBRICS AS A TEACHING TOOL FOR STUDENTS

Eventually, I stumbled across the process I'd been looking for. In his *Teaching Adolescent Writers* (2006), English teacher Kelly Gallagher describes a way to use rubrics as a teaching tool. First, the teacher collects drafts of an assigned essay and evaluates them. After discerning a few problematic issues common to most of the essays, the teacher selects a few exemplary papers and shows these to students so that they might discern the difference between their essays and the exemplary ones. The teacher then elicits observations from the students about what results in poor, good, and excellent quality and uses those observations to generate a rubric for the assignment. Finally, students revise their essays, which are then graded for just the issues covered in class (pp. 154-159).

Of course, a homeschooling educator can't repeat Gallagher's process exactly, but I saw much in the process that any teacher could apply:

- Issues in students' actual writing determine objectives and grading criteria
- Students observe what constitutes quality for themselves
- Descriptions for each criterion distinguish writing that meets the standard, exceeds the standard, and does not yet meet the standard
- Distinctions in quality become evident and objective to students

This last item is particularly important, because it means that the process essentially eliminates the possibility of that red pen approach to grading that so discourages students. A rubric that targets the specific skills students are learning and clearly identifies the quality students are trying to achieve guides writing and brings students into the evaluation process. The consistent use of tailored rubrics actually empowers students to master the many criteria that make up good writing.

And consistency is a critical factor here. Although the process described above applied to isolated essays, applying a rubric to multiple projects over an extended period of time renders greater benefit. According to education professor Ralph Tyler (1949), grading isolated products has little or no value for evaluating progress toward goals:

> The conception of evaluation has two important aspects. In the first place, it implies that evaluation must appraise the behavior of students since it is change in these behaviors which is sought in education. In the second place, it implies that *evaluation must involve more than a single appraisal* at any one time since to see whether change has taken place, it is necessary to make an appraisal at an early point and other appraisals at later points to identify changes that may be occurring. On this basis, one is not able to evaluate an instructional program by testing students only at the end of the program. Without knowing where the students were at the beginning, it is not possible to tell how far changes have taken place. (p. 106, emphasis mine)

Most high school composition programs fail to consider Tyler's point. Generally, English teachers assign diverse writing projects and grade them in isolation from one another. As a result, grades cannot and do not measure learning or growth; students who have not learned anything may score high or low, depending on their ability and their assessor's appraisal. Students may get practice writing for diverse purposes as the content standards require, but unless they have innate ability, they neither get good grades nor learn how to write any better.

A composition program should not merely reward students with innate ability and discourage those without; it should foster growth in every student. As much as possible, students of writing should stick to a single form, purpose, and tone while learning to apply qualities of good writing. In this way, students are allowed to focus on the objectives they need to learn and gradually attain them, rather than continually attempting diverse projects involving new forms and tones but perfecting none. "Connectedness in growth" John Dewey writes, "must be [the educator's] constant watchword" (1938, p. 75).

Growth comes from practicing the same skills over time; it is measured by evaluating efforts with the same tool. That's where the use of a consistent individualized rubric over time becomes indispensable. It serves as a measurement tool that allows teachers to provide real feedback to students and encourage real growth. Students not only have the opportunity to revise a particular essay for a particular issue, but to consistently apply skills that result in higher quality and which become ingrained and pervade all subsequent writing.

Designing an Individualized Rubric

But what does all of this look like in a homeschool setting? As you can probably tell, although this approach simplifies many aspects of teaching composition, it does require some setting up. Basically, you need to make sure your student understands a specific form—namely, the five-paragraph essay taught in the next chapter—and a limited number of developmentally appropriate writing tasks, which I will explain in Chapter 5. These are prerequisites to the rubric generation process. Once your student understands how to compose a basic five-paragraph essay, you'll need to assess the quality of what he or she can capably produce.

Now, you might devise an individualized rubric for your student autonomously, based on goals that you have for your student or maybe based on errors you have seen in your student's writing. Assuming you explained the objectives identified on the rubric and showed your student how they translate into a grade, it would work. Still, I would encourage you to involve your student in this process. Not only will your student feel more ownership over his or her writing, but the process of analyzing and evaluating essays actually teaches students what constitutes quality more effectively than lectures or worksheets can do.

1. Understand What Constitutes Quality

First, take time to familiarize yourself with what constitutes quality. As I have already argued, the most important quality in academic writing is clarity, followed by coherence and eloquence. Chapters 6 – 8 each identify three specific factors that affect each of these qualities, typical points of confusion for students, as well as advice for resolving issues. For instance, Chapter 6 describes what you should look for in your student's essay in terms of adequate content, sentence structure, and writing conventions. The chapter also provides diagnostic tools, such as a rubric on page 73 and a checklist on page 74, to help you determine which issues are most prevalent in your student's writing. Not only do Chapters 6 – 8 describe common problems, they also explain why certain patterns are problematic and show how to fix them. Gaining familiarity with these issues will help you suggest a limited number of doable, objective goals that will have the greatest impact on your student's writing in the least amount of time.

2. Get a Writing Sample

The next step in this process is getting an initial assessment of the student's writing. There is no point in working on objectives that your student has already mastered or that your student is not ready for. So before you can work with your student to identify what will improve the quality of his or her writing, you need to evaluate the student's actual writing so that you can prioritize and focus on the specific issues your student is struggling with most.

Give your student a prompt for a five-paragraph essay that doesn't present too much challenge—say, one that touches on an area of particular interest. Appropriate prompts might include something like one of these:

- What are the benefits of participating in [some sport or leisure activity]?
- What is a pet peeve? Describe three of yours.
- What genres make the best books (or movies), and why do you think so?
- What are the steps involved in getting your driver's license?
- Should teachers assign more homework—why or why not?
- Why might people become involved in an online community?

Whatever your prompt, make sure it is one that your student can write about fairly easily, conducting little or no research. The content of this essay doesn't need to be scholarly; the point of the exercise is to demonstrate the quality of writing your student can produce.

Ask your student to write this essay using a five-paragraph model, with one paragraph dedicated to an introduction, three paragraphs in the body of the essay, and another paragraph for the conclusion. If you have any doubts about explaining a five-paragraph essay, see Chapter 4. Handouts and templates for planning a five-paragraph essay and developing paragraphs can be found in Appendices B, C and E; Appendix D contains several sample five-paragraph essays.

Make sure to give your student enough time to write the essay, set it aside, and then return to the essay with fresh eyes to critically review and edit. You want your assessment to be based on the quality of writing your student can capably produce, so clarify that you expect this essay to be revised and edited before the assessment session. Since no research is involved, a week should give most students ample time to complete this assignment.

3. Generate a Model for Comparison

Next, write an essay on the same or a similar topic as your student yourself. You may cringe at this idea, but writing with your student serves several purposes. First, it puts many students at ease to write alongside another writer. Second, it'll remind you how hard it is to write an academic essay, which, if you're like most people, you won't have done for a while. Most importantly, it generates a second essay against which your student can compare his or her efforts. Comparing two essays helps students discern what otherwise might go unnoticed. For instance, a student who writes a paragraph of only a couple of sentences might consider the paragraph complete simply because he or she had nothing else to say. Comparing such a short paragraph against a substantially more developed one might suggest to the student a few ideas about how he or she might add more details in the future.

Don't worry about composing a perfect or exemplary essay yourself. Mine never are. In any case, the goal for students is not perfection but improvement. You don't want your essay to intimidate your student but rather to provide contrast. In some ways, your student's essay may actually be better than yours. If that happens, great! Your student will love that.

If you really you don't want to write an essay, you do have a few options that will allow your student to compare his or her essay with a similar one. The first option would be to recruit a peer to participate in this process with you. Another would be to assign one of the prompts used for the sample essays in Appendix D of this book. Specifically, appropriate prompts for this initial essay include the following:

- What are the best kinds of spectator sports (or books or movies or vacations)?

- How do you make cookies (or another familiar process)?
- Read A.A. Milne's short story, "In Which Rabbit Has a Busy Day and We Find out What Christopher Robin Does in the Mornings" (currently accessible online at http://www.lib.ru/MILN/pooh2.txt) and answer the question: What are the various animals' attitudes about education, and which do you think is the best to have?

4. Swap Papers and Discuss Merits

Fourth, assuming you have two or more essays to compare, swap papers and discuss what each of the essays did well and what each might have done better. Consider especially how well each essay answers the prompt. Make sure you find a few things to appreciate in your student's writing. Even an essay riddled with errors will often contain good ideas. Emphasize the fact that good ideas deserve to be understood by readers, and that learning to write better will help your student communicate his or her good ideas more effectively.

5. Discern Areas of Weakness

After discussing the essays, use the included rubrics to guide your analysis and decide which aspect of your student's writing most needs improving. The rubrics in Chapters 6 – 8 each identify six broad criteria outlining what specifically results in quality essays. For instance, the first quality for which you will evaluate your student's essay will be clear content. The rubric on page 73 identifies 'Introduction Content' as one criterion for quality in an academic essay, and it indicates that an adequate essay will contain a context for the essay topic and a thesis statement that answers the academic prompt, while an excellent essay will contain a context, answer, and a "hook." An essay lacking an adequate introduction will be missing one of the two essential ingredients, either a context or an answer to the prompt.

By circling which description best describes each aspect of the essay on this rubric, you can discern which issues most affect the overall quality of your student's writing. Since the purpose of this activity is to identify goals for your student, you will probably find that your student's writing falls in the 'unacceptable' category for many of the criteria. Remind your student that this is okay; in fact, it's the whole point of this activity. By pinpointing what needs work, students can improve the quality of their writing overall.

So that this exercise does not become overwhelmingly negative, limit your observations to no more than three or four problem areas. For instance, if the initial assessment of a student's essay reveals that content is lacking in the introduction, body, and conclusion (the first three criteria on the clear content rubric), it should be obvious that developing each of these need to be prioritized on that student's individualized rubric: an essay needs content before that content can be clarified.

6. Analyze Each of the Problem Issues and Generate Objectives

In order to design a useful rubric, you must not only identify weaknesses; you must also analyze them. What specifically prevents your student from performing adequately on a low-scoring criterion? For instance, if your student's introduction content scores low, determine why. Did the student include no introduction at all? Did the student fail to provide any context so that the reader initially has no idea what the essay was about? Did the student include no thesis statement?

Remember, this rubric relies on objective, observable data. "Your introduction was off" is unhelpful feedback; "Your introduction provides no context" tells students what needs to be revised in future attempts. In order to help your student improve his or her writing, you must identify the specific issues that emerged on the practice essay, list them as criteria on the individualized rubric, and describe exactly what the student needs to do in order to perform better in the future.

For instance, say your student's writing is sometimes confusing because some sentences lack punctuation. Okay: now ask, what kind of punctuation is lacking? It is not enough to tell students to punctuate correctly. I have found this to be especially true with commas. You must identify specifically where the confusion lies, explain the rationale behind whatever rule students don't understand, and make it a goal for them to focus on correcting that rule in future efforts. Students flustered by many rules feel empowered when asked to take responsibility for correcting just one or two at a time.

Often, the exercise of figuring out what needs improving effectively explains to students the concepts they need to learn. Maybe your student didn't understand the function of topic sentences in a paragraph or how to generate one successfully. No problem: add the item to his or her personal rubric, provide some instruction about topic sentences, and have your student describe the difference between good, excellent, and poor topic sentences on the rubric. Then, expect stellar topic sentences in the next essay.

Or say your student's paper contained errors in capitalization. You and your student might decide to identify capitalization as one criterion on the individualized rubric.

Criteria	Unacceptable; needs revision	Acceptable; meets the standard	Excellent; exceeds the standard
Conventions: Capitalization			

Next, you would analyze when and why the errors were made. For instance, maybe the student failed to capitalize 'Civil War' as well as the title 'President' before Abraham Lincoln.' Those errors would tell you specifically which capitalization rules to apply in future essays: (1) capitalize proper nouns and (2) capitalize titles when they precede proper nouns. Write down what proper capitalization looks like in the "acceptable" category:

Category & Criteria	Unacceptable; needs revision	Acceptable; meets the standard	Excellent; exceeds the standard
Conventions: Capitalization		The writer capitalizes titles when they precede proper nouns and proper nouns that name specific people, places, things, or events	

After describing what correct capitalization looks like, decide what is the absolute minimum standard of correctness you would accept for this criterion. What does the writing of a student who understands the rules of capitalization look like? A student who produces an essay containing twenty errors obviously does not "get it." But what about an essay with one error? Does that student get it? Probably. One error is probably just a mistake. Now, whether two, three, or just one error constitutes 'acceptable' is up to you (and, to a lesser degree, your student); I would, however, suggest that expecting zero errors would not be an appropriate minimum standard for any criterion; rather, reserve perfection for the "exceeds the standard" category:

Category & Criteria	Unacceptable; needs revision	Acceptable; meets the standard	Excellent; exceeds the standard
Conventions: Capitalization		The writer capitalizes titles when they precede proper nouns and proper nouns that name specific people, places, things, or events with no more than one error per page	The writer capitalizes titles when they precede proper nouns and proper nouns that name specific people, places, things, or events (no errors)

That leaves the "needs revision" category, which your student should be able to infer by considering what meets the standard. Students should be able to independently fill in this description: either 'the writer fails to capitalize words as described in the 'meeting the standards' category' or 'the writer exceeds the permitted number of errors for the criterion.'

Category & Criteria	Unacceptable; needs revision	Acceptable; meets the standard	Excellent; exceeds the standard
Conventions: Capitalization	The writer does not capitalize proper nouns or titles preceding proper nouns in two or more instances per page	The writer capitalizes proper nouns that identify specific people, places, things, or events and titles preceding proper nouns with no more than one error per page	The writer capitalizes proper nouns and titles preceding proper nouns, making no errors in the essay

Repeat the same process with each of the criteria you want to focus on for the duration of the grading period. Always begin with the basic, 'meets the standard' category: this is the box where you clarify exactly what your student needs to learn. Conclude with the 'needs revision' category, which reinforces the lesson. Also, if possible, have your student write out the descriptions you agree upon even if his or her handwriting is sloppy; writing each principle also reinforces learning. You or your student can always produce a neater rubric on a computer later.

7. Target Problem Issues while Retaining Broad Objectives

Each individualized rubric you generate targets just six objectives that your student will retain over a significant period of time. You may be tempted to fill the entire rubric with objectives that focus on just one issue that you perceive as severe; however, each rubric should ideally identify a balanced set of objectives in order to remind students to produce well-rounded essays.

You will notice also that the rubrics for each subsequent level in the program retain broad criteria for previous levels. This is purposeful; it reminds students that each quality must be retained even as they move on to new qualities and new objectives. For instance, the rubric for coherence incorporates the objectives of answering the essay prompt with clearly written sentences, which makes sense because no essay can be considered coherent that does not first contain clear content: coherence is essentially a matter of organizing clear and meaningful sentences. So every rubric you generate will include an increasing number of broad criteria that remind students to retain previously learned qualities and gradually decreasing numbers of goals focusing on specific issues to revise.

USING THE RUBRIC TO ASSESS PROGRESS

Unlike a rubric attached to a specific assignment, a consistent rubric outlining individualized goals helps students cement writing skills and resolve persistent problems. Because the rubric stays the same, students know what to watch out for and revise. Problem issues cease to resurface continually; rather, they fade out gradually until they disappear altogether.

Depending on how quickly your student masters the goals set by his or her individualized rubric, you might retain one or all of the same objectives over the course of a quarter, a semester, or even an entire academic year. Should your student's scores on the essays fall or plateau, review the goals with your student and try to learn where the confusion lies. You may have to re-teach a concept or clarify what a sentence or paragraph should look like. If your student continues to struggle, consider going over drafts of essays and revising problem areas together until your student understands the skill and can perform it independently.

A single, consistent rubric allows you to chart growth. A simple way of scoring any assignment using a rubric is to assign a point-value to each level of achievement. For instance, the rubric might give the student zero points for falling in the 'unacceptable' or 'inadequate' category, one point for 'acceptable' content, and two points for 'excellent' work. Since the rubric includes six criteria, the total number of points available for an essay that excels in every possible way will be twelve. Of course, you can assign higher numbers— one, three, and five, perhaps—so that you have more wiggle room in grading. Although you want grading to be as impartial as possible, some objectives may be less clear-cut. For instance, a student's score may fall between categories on an objective like body paragraph content, in which one paragraph may be excellent while another paragraph is just so-so. In that case, a score of 4—between adequate and excellent—makes sense.

To score any essay, simply divide the points earned by the total possible. An essay that earns seven out of twelve points earns 58%. Now, a 58 might sound like a terrible score for any assignment, but remember that a student who earns 100% on the first attempt has nowhere to go in terms of progress. You want the criteria on a rubric to address skills and issues that your student needs to master, not the ones that he or she has already learned. Therefore, you should expect students to earn low scores on the first essays graded with a particular individualized rubric, and scores should gradually rise as students master each of the rubric's six objectives. Eventually, your student's scores should be consistently in the 90's.

That means that an 'A' in this course won't reflect consistent A's on every essay from first to last. A writing class in which students can earn consistent A's might make it easy for a teacher to dole out straight A's, but such a class reveals little about how much progress a student has made in any particular aspect of writing—and, in effect, a student may not have made any progress at all. In my opinion, a writing course that does not help students write with increasing competence offers little benefit to students. So success in this course will not look like a string of 90's in your grade book. Success will look like scores that start around 50 or 60 and gradually move up to the 90's.

ASSIGNING GRADES

How you want to assign a grade for this course is ultimately up to you, but I would suggest that the grade your student receives for composition should reflect what he or she has achieved. Now, math is not my strong suit, but I'm pretty sure that averaging numbers that go from scores in the 50's up to scores in the 90's will never average out at 90 or above, or an A. But students who have made remarkable progress toward composing high quality essays deserve an A—just as a student who has done the work but made no progress deserves a D—the lowest passing grade.

If you want to tie those grades to numbers and keep this objective, take the scores from all of the student's essays in a grading period and list them in order. If the goals were appropriate, if you and your student used the rubric consistently to evaluate those essays, and if you addressed persistent issues with extra lessons, those numbers should have gradually increased over time.

Following the rationale for grading above, then, an increase of ten percentage points (from a 67 to a 77, for instance) over the grading period (from the first graded essay to the last) would indicate some progress toward goals. Assuming scores are fairly consistent and all fall between those two numbers, the student will have made adequate progress: the grade for an increase of ten points is a C. An increase of twenty points (from a 67 to an 87, for instance) would constitute a B. An increase of thirty or more (from a 67 to a 97, for instance) would constitute an A.

To show you how this grading strategy differs from the typical one, compare this scorebook, which shows the grade derived by averaging the scores of essays written over the course of a grading period:

Essay	1	2	3	4	5	6	7	Average	Grade
Score	52	71	75	83	87	92	95	79	C+

Assuming that those scores are based on a single set of grading criteria, what they reflect is real growth in the student's abilities, which should translate into a good grade, not a mediocre one. Now, consider the difference when the same scores are not averaged, but evaluated for progress:

Essay	1	2	3	4	5	6	7	Increase	Grade
Score	52	71	75	83	87	92	95	43	A+

APPARENT GROWTH

Your student's growth in this program should be apparent. Not only should you be able to point to numbers that show progress, you should be able to place the student's initial composition side-by-side with the final one for the grading period and see marked improvement. Not only should you see the improvement, your student should see improvement. Other people should be able to see it, too. The first time I tried using a consistent rubric, I had our advisor compare Kristen's first and last essays. He glanced at the first one, skimmed a bit, and frowned a little. Then he flipped to the final essay Kristen had written. He read a few lines, sat up straight, and said, "Oh, yeah. This one is a lot better."

Of course, the reason it was so easy to observe this growth is that the form and purpose in both of the compositions were consistent. The rubric would have been significantly less useful had the first assignment consisted of a position paper and subsequent assignments consisted of an analysis, a short story, a personal reflection, a research paper, and a haiku. Such a course might provide a student broader exposure to writing purposes and tasks, but it would not allow the student to focus or develop any particular quality to speak of. If a student of any complicated endeavor is to improve his or her skill, consistent focus and practice is essential.

The Problem with Holistic Assessments

Now, focusing on specific issues in your student's writing means that you should see improvement in those areas, but don't expect your student's writing to improve in every area. An individualized rubric will not result in immediate growth if submitted to a comprehensive or holistic assessment; in fact, odds are good that as a whole, your student's writing will actually get slightly worse.

Let me give you an example of what I mean here. The first quality I suggest students learn is that of conveying substantial content clearly. So say that your student learns to revise his or her sentences to prioritize clear subjects and active verbs. That's excellent! Unfortunately, when you ask a student to write clearly this way, you are asking your student to take the natural way he or she has constructed a sentence, which is probably akin to the way your student normally thinks and talks, and substitute a less natural but more effective construction. This substitution has consequences, the most immediate of which is that your student's writing may seem choppier than before.

This is an instance of tearing something apart to make it better. Just as re-decorating the living room is going to make that space unlivable until you finish making improvements, sometimes re-training a student's writing process to include revising sentences for clarity temporarily detracts from overall eloquence. This regression, however, does not last; it merely reflects this stage in the process.

A second and less immediate consequence of your student developing clarity in writing is improved communication skills in general. Students who regularly discipline themselves to choose words with care tend to communicate more precisely and more concisely than other people. You will notice them not only writing more effectively, but often they will begin to use words artfully, both orally and in writing. They may not make the connection, but students who prioritize the qualities of clarity, coherence, and eloquence in writing often develop the ability to display them in conversation as well.

So don't be deterred from the process. Others may pressure you to teach your student to write compositions with more voice or variety or creativity or style. Certainly, do not discourage your student if he or she independently composes pieces that demonstrate these qualities, but do not allow these less important qualities to take precedence in your student's composition course. The ability to draft and revise sentences to have clear subjects and active verbs or to ensure a tightly coherent argument takes time to develop. Students who are not allowed to focus on these difficult skills never really learn them well. They learn only to get by as writers and never develop the quick wit and precise responses of great communicators.

Putting the Rubric into Practice

Once your student has an individualized rubric, supply him or her with a set of rubrics and start assigning essays. For many students, an essay every week is an appropriate amount of practice; a few students do better with bi-weekly assignments.

How often you evaluate essays is up to you. Initially, it's best to evaluate each essay right away so that any confusion about the objectives may be resolved. You can do this independently and go over your assessment with your student afterwards; alternatively, you can evaluate essays together. After a few trials, however, you may postpone evaluation sessions for a few weeks and schedule a larger block of time to go over three or four essays at once. Do not, however, hold off evaluation sessions until the end of the grading session.

Using the individualized rubric will make evaluating your student's essays relatively straight-forward and much more objective. You will need to make several copies of the rubric so that you can attach one to each essay. Then, when you evaluate each essay, simply circle the description for each criterion that best reflects the student's writing. If you have been clear in your descriptions, there should be little subjectivity involved in this. Are there zero errors in capitalization? Circle 'excellent' and move on to the next criterion. Both you and your student should be able to see why the essay gets the score it does.

It is a good idea to permit your student to make revisions on a low scoring essay—or any essay, for that matter—if he or she wants to. Making corrections and improvements can only reinforce the lessons your student needs to learn. Eventually, your student will have learned and corrected all of the issues on the rubric and be ready to tackle new challenges in his or her writing.

Chapter 4

Consistent Form

The most valuable thing I learned in high school was how to write a five-paragraph essay. Now, that's not to say that I had fun learning that skill. The truth is, learning to write a decent essay was hard and, as I recall, frustrating. Even though I really liked my teacher, I dreaded the many writing assignments he gave out almost as much as I dreaded the critical feedback I knew I'd get when I got my essays back. Getting an A out of Mr. Hartman was a rare occurrence. But when I enrolled in college, I remember finding the many timed essay tests much easier than most of my peers, who hated taking them and complained about their grades when they got them back. I soon realized that Mr. Hartman had done me a favor by continually assigning five-paragraph essays.

Some English teachers no longer give priority to teaching the five-paragraph essay, claiming that students shouldn't "try to stuff ideas into predetermined boxes of form" but rather "allow form to emerge naturally" (Noden, 1999, p. 174-175). Noden (1999) points to the experience of author Russell Baker, who deviated from the prescribed five-paragraph form and won the approval of his peers: "Suddenly," Baker writes, "I wanted to write about the warmth and good feeling of [my family eating spaghetti], but I wanted to put it down simply for my own joy, not for Mr. Fleagle" (as cited in Noden, p. 175). The humorous essay Baker wrote so impressed his teacher that he praised the essay and read it out loud to the entire class. The anecdote seems to support the notion that five-paragraph essays stifle young writers, but I'm not so sure: what the teacher who cites this incident doesn't seem to notice is that the writer in this story abandoned the five-paragraph form only *after he had learned to write by using it*. Would he have been as successful if he had not? No one knows.

What I do know is that students who graduate from high school without learning to write a five-paragraph essay are at a disadvantage in college. More than one shell-shocked student has come to me, distraught because they're out of their depths in a basic college or remedial writing class—sometimes in spite of getting straight A's on writing assignments in high school.

Of course, the five-paragraph essay form is not the only form with which to write, and it's true that most professional writers don't follow it. But its formulaic nature is a good thing for beginning writers who are learning to organize and express ideas skillfully. The consistent form that the five-paragraph essay provides allows students to focus on expressing good ideas well, without worrying about organization or formatting. What's more, most timed testing situations in high school and college call for the ability to write a five-paragraph essay on demand. Finally, the five-paragraph form trains students to appreciate the rhetorical power of thinking in threes by requiring three supporting paragraphs. Training students to develop five-paragraph essays in response to academic prompts only serves them in the end.

In this chapter, I'm going to suggest that you retain the five-paragraph essay form and challenge your student to compose essays using it regularly for at least the first two years of high school. Then, or at some later point (depending on the student), students who are ready to write research papers and arguments will expand upon this five-paragraph form by adopting the argument form, which coincidentally also contains five sections, or by applying arbitrary paragraphing to their writing.

BASIC FIVE-PARAGRAPH ESSAY FORM

Somewhat obviously, a five-paragraph essay contains five paragraphs: a paragraph that introduces the topic, three body paragraphs which develop the student's ideas about that topic, and a paragraph for conclusion. High school students who have experience writing essays will probably be both familiar and comfortable with the five-paragraph format, but students new to essay writing will need some information about the three paragraph types as well as strategies for composing each type of paragraph.

The text boxes on the next page indicate what kind of content goes into each of these paragraphs. In addition, handouts for students who need help developing a paragraph can be found in Appendix C. For students who wish to see a sample five-paragraph essay, see Appendix D. Finally, more detailed information about what kind of content pertains to each of the three types of paragraphs in a five-paragraph essay can be found in Chapter 6.

Paragraph Functions in a Five-Paragraph Essay

Introduction Paragraph

- Introduces the essay topic, either generally or in an intriguing way
- Provides a context for the essay or comments on the topic
- Ends with an announcement of the writer's intent or a thesis statement

---

Body Paragraph 1

- Develops the student's first answer, the first part of an answer, or the first point in answer to the academic prompt
- Begins with a topic sentence
- Supports the topic sentence with clarifying explanations, analogies, or examples and includes explanatory details about them

---

Body Paragraph 2

- Develops the student's second answer, the second part of an answer, or the second point in answer to the academic prompt
- Begins with a topic sentence
- Supports the topic sentence with clarifying explanations, analogies, or examples and includes explanatory details about them

---

Body Paragraph 3

- Develops the student's third answer, the third part of an answer, or the third point in answer to the academic prompt
- Begins with a topic sentence
- Supports the topic sentence with clarifying explanations, analogies, or examples and includes explanatory details about them

---

Conclusion Paragraph

- Reiterates main points of essay without repeating them verbatim
- Draws a conclusion, identifies a pertinent implication, or evaluates the issue
- Concludes on a resonant note

Developing Paragraphs

If an essay lacks content, either in terms of a clear thesis statement or in terms of substantive support, try talking to your student about the prompt, clarifying that you only want a brief answer, as in a single sentence. Sometimes, the pressure to seem smart on paper stifles students so much that they feel like they have nothing to say. Talking about the topic often relaxes such students, and by hearing what your student thinks, you can determine if your student is struggling with understanding the topic or just writing about it. If understanding is not a problem, try writing down the substantive ideas your student says. Sometimes, seeing words on paper conveying ideas clearly is all it takes for a student to say, "Oh, I see. I just need to write what I think."

Students who are struggling to understand their essay topic will need to go back to their source. If this source includes a list of key terms, it may help to have your student copy these down. Then, have your student create three columns on a piece of paper and label one 'actors,' one 'actions,' and one 'concepts.' Under the 'actors' label, ask your student to list the people or things that do something or make things happen in the text. Under 'actions,' ask the student to write down the verbs that describe what the actors do or what happens in the text. Finally, under 'concepts,' ask your student to write down the other important words in the reading. These words should provide a good portion of the vocabulary your student will need in order to compose an essay.

Consider also utilizing graphic organizers to help your student see how the main actors, actions, and concepts are related. Graphic organizers help students assimilate new information and retain material (Irwin-DeVitis, Bromley, & Modlo, 1999, p. 6). A good resource for students who need to see information in order to understand it is Inspiration software, which not only allows students to graphically organize information using a computer, but also converts the information into an outline from which to write.

FACILITATING ESSAY WRITING FOR ANXIOUS OR DISCOURAGED STUDENTS

Students who become very anxious when faced with the prospect of writing an essay and students who insist that they can't write, period, may need to have the five-paragraph form temporarily divided up and parceled out in stages. Instead of giving your student a prompt and expecting him or her to write an entire essay independently, walk your student through the process of planning an essay in response to a prompt. Do this orally, without asking the student to write anything down. Just letting your student talk through the main points of a response to a prompt goes a long way toward easing anxiety about writing. The paragraphs below describe in more detail how to walk an anxious student through the planning and drafting of an initial essay.

1. Choose a suitable prompt.

The simplest writing tasks involve conveying information. For a student attempting his or her first essay, I try to stick with a prompt that requires the student to convey information that either interests or appeals to them. Prompts that elicit information might touch on their studies or hobbies, as in 'What made the ancient Egyptians so fascinating?' or 'What different kinds of books do you find most appealing?' Another type of prompt asks the student to describe a process, as in 'How does one go about sewing a dress?' or 'How would you teach someone else to play the guitar?' Throw out a couple of possibilities and let your student choose between them.

At the high school level, academic topics are generally most appropriate; still, most students do best with familiar topics for their initial attempts. Be careful, however, to suggest topics that not mundane. I know one high school student who complained that she'd been assigned an essay about brushing her teeth, and she had a real point—the essay topic was clearly designed to get her to write something, no matter how inane. Most students don't feel such essays are worth writing. Instead, suggest a few possibilities for essay prompts about which the student is uniquely knowledgeable. For example, one of the girls I tutor raises prize-winning hogs. I asked her to write about what she did to be so successful. Another student played guitar, and I asked him to tell me how he learned to play so well. Because the prompts allowed these students to communicate something they cared about, they didn't mind writing.

Another possibility is to suggest students write about something that intrigues them. I call this the 'Curiosity topic.' Sort of an intermediary category between familiar and academic topics, curiosity essays invite students to write about something about which they have always been curious or something which recently piqued their interest, if only briefly. An example of the former might be, "Why is the sky blue?" or "How does TV work?" An example of the latter could be about anything that the student comes across that suddenly seems interesting: "What do they put in Vitamin Enhanced Water?" or "Whatever happened to Hannah Montana?" This kind of essay requires some research, but not much. Wikipedia is great for not-quite-academic topics like these, and even reluctant students may enjoy writing essays that allow them to explore their own interests.

2. **Ask the student to generate 3 answers.**

    Once you have a prompt for the essay, walk your student through the process of choosing a distinct focus for each of three body paragraphs. First, have your student write the prompt across the top of a page and the numbers one through three down the side of the page, in the margin. Next, ask your student how he or she would answer the academic prompt in a few words or a single sentence. Accept any response that answers the academic prompt and suggest your student write the gist of it on the page next to one of the numbers. Then, depending on the prompt, ask either, "What else?" or "What next?" Soon, your student will have three ideas about how to answer the essay prompt. Written as complete sentences, these become topic sentences from which your student can develop a thesis statement and three body paragraphs. In short, just by talking about the prompt, the student can get a basic plan for writing the essay.

    For instance, say you and your student agree on an essay topic of "good movies." Great: next, find an angle that breaks that topic up into three categories. One way to do that—although I'm sure there are others—is to define categories that are abstract enough to allow exemplification: What qualities make for good movies? Most students can easily name a few qualities they like in movies: maybe they're exciting or funny, gory or sad, scary or beautiful or romantic or thought-provoking. After picking the three top qualities that make movies good, ask your student to write a simple sentence stating as much: "One quality that makes a movie good is humor." Have your student repeat the exercise for the other two qualities ("Another quality in good movies is X"; "A third quality is Y"); then, discuss options for elaborating on those assertions.

3. **Develop one of the body paragraphs together.**

    Most students will probably sense a need to suggest examples here, and exemplification is always a good bet when dealing with abstract ideas, since abstract concepts exist only in the examples that make them up. In other words, the abstract concept of humor is not something you can see or touch, but when humor happens, you know it because you laugh. Humor, then, is the concept someone made up to describe all situations involving humor; that is how concepts like humor get their definitions. So examples are a great way to support assertions involving abstraction: "For instance, the movie, 'The Princess Bride' is a great movie because it is funny." Then, if your student doesn't automatically think of it, suggest adding a few supporting details: "When the man in black climbs up the cliff, the swordsman gets impatient and urges the man in black to hurry up. It's funny because the man in black knows that the swordsman means to kill him, and most people are in no hurry to die." Have your student write down the sentences he or she suggests. As long as the sentences are mostly coherent, don't worry about nit-picking spelling or grammar—you want your student to feel capable of composing a simple paragraph. Perfecting comes later.

5. **Consider taking dictation.**

Sometimes, students convinced of their inability to write need to see their ideas transposed onto paper. For these students, it is sometimes a good idea to write down what they say as they say it. In other words, you might take dictation as your student responds to your questions about how he or she would respond to a prompt or support an assertion. As a writing tutor, I do this a lot, especially for students whose writing I'm seeing as largely incoherent but whose speech is not. These students often have two issues going on. First, they are smarter than they feel, and because they can see perfectly well that their writing doesn't do their ideas justice, they conclude that they can't write. This is not the case—I've seen student after student watch their ideas come to life on paper, and many of them become instant converts when they see what they need to do to: first get the concept on the paper and then re-work it until it's clear.

Another issue for many students is that they think faster than they can write. And, while this is true for most people, there is a real difference in how quickly people can transpose ideas to paper. I happen to type about 70 words per minute. My typing speed facilitates my ability to get my ideas down on paper before I forget them. Some students chicken peck at about 15 to 20 words per minute, and some less. That's a huge difference. What these students need is some acknowledgement—"yes, it's very frustrating that your ideas fly faster than your fingers"—and some encouragement: "Nevertheless, your ideas are worth preserving. Take time to capture the main ideas—which are your topic sentences and thesis statement—as clearly as possible. Once you get the essential ideas down, the rest will fall into place."

6. **Try writing sentences first.**

Another way to help students get accustomed to writing a single paragraph is to make writing a paragraph feel like writing sentences. Have your student write a prompt across the top of a page and then number every other line down the left side of a piece of paper from one to ten. Then ask your student to write ten short and simple sentences that support the topic sentence written across the top of the page. Limiting the length and complexity of the sentences sometimes helps reduce anxiety for students and allows them to get basic ideas out on paper. Once the student has written the ten simple sentences, consider whether any sentences need to be eliminated because they don't quite fit the topic, as well as which sentences might be combined. Combining the simple sentences is what will turn what now feels like a collection of choppy sentences into a single, eloquent set.

Beginning with the topic sentence, compose the paragraph by piecing together the sentences. You might suggest a few transitional phrases or ways to combine sentences to vary the lengths of sentences in order to improve the paragraph's flow, but don't take over the process; treat it as more of a joint experiment. Your student should see that writing is a process of trial and error. Watching someone else struggle to put ideas together in the best possible way goes a long way toward convincing students who think they can't write just because they can't get their words to come out right the first time around that it's okay to have to write and re-write a paragraph. In fact, it's normal. (I doubt there is even one paragraph in this book that I didn't re-write at least three times before considering it done.)

7. Downplay the drama.

I downplay the introduction and conclusion for students who are first getting used to writing essays. Students who feel insecure writing feel especially intimidated by the challenges of "hooking" a reader and sounding conclusive—and rightfully so. Introductions and conclusions are the most difficult parts of an essay to write well, which is why I suggest emphasizing the body paragraphs first and requiring only the most basic content of introductions and conclusions initially. Postpone evaluating introductions and conclusions for rhetorical strength until later.

How Long Must Students Retain the Five-Paragraph Essay Form?

Many students will feel comfortable writing five-paragraphs and be ready to move on to more expansive compositions after about two years of consistent practice. If writing is a regular part of their school week, most students will have written more than fifty essays by that time. That number may seem daunting, but remember that students may apply their writing to any subject, be it history, economics, government, biology, physics, philosophy, health, or literature, and writing assignments can replace regular worksheet exercises, special projects, and even unit tests. When you assign essays on a regular basis, believe me, they add up fast. Not only do students get all the practice they need with writing, you get all the documentation you need to prove your student is learning history, science, health, or whatever—on top of composition.

Backtracking: On Assigning Paragraphs

Although composing five-paragraph essays is an important objective for high school students, not every writing assignment needs to be a complete essay. Many of the summary and review prompts included in textbooks for subjects like science, health, government, and history are designed to be satisfactorily answered with a paragraph. These present an excellent opportunity for students to cement their knowledge in these subjects while simultaneously practicing writing with the qualities they are learning for composition. So long as students also get regular practice composing five-paragraph essays, it makes a lot of sense to apply those paragraphs to the requirements of the composition course and evaluate them using the same individualized rubric, excepting, of course, any criteria that specifically apply to the five-paragraph form.

Deviating from the Five-Paragraph Essay Form

Before wrapping up this section, I would only add that students should understand that they do have the freedom to modify the five-paragraph form if necessary. For instance, sometimes a student will only be able to think of two good reasons for some phenomenon. Fine: eliminate one of the three body paragraphs and write a four-paragraph essay. Other times, a student will want to develop a fourth body paragraph—again, no problem. There's nothing magic about the number five except that it gives students something firm to hold in mind and shoot for as they learn to compose basic essays.

Once your student is familiar with the five-paragraph essay form, you can proceed to giving your student regular academic prompts, starting with the simplest writing tasks and gradually progressing toward more advanced ones. The next chapter will discuss the order of these writing purposes; for now, I would only reiterate that the basic five-paragraph form will accommodate any of them and that retaining it as your student practices writing for increasingly challenging purposes will allow your student to focus on writing for each specific purpose with the specific quality he or she is attempting to learn.

Chapter 5

Fundamental Purposes

Not long ago, a college student asked me to give him feedback on an essay he'd written. The essay contained an interesting array of experiences and observations the writer had had while traveling abroad. In the first paragraph, he described a ruin in the Middle East where he had camped out. The descriptions in the first paragraph were certainly intriguing, but the second paragraph went in another direction, and so did the third. In fact, the piece was all over the place: sometimes thought-provoking, sometimes humorous, sometimes inflammatory. I found I couldn't get interested in the essay because I didn't know whether I was supposed to be informed, included, entertained, or persuaded. In spite of reasonably good writing quality, the lack of clear purpose put me off, and from the second paragraph on, I just wanted to stop reading.

Having a clear purpose matters. What confuses many students is that many writers these days don't have one, and some of them write well in spite of it. A lot of bloggers, for instance, kind of ramble on, and some of them draw an audience who enjoy their ramblings. Also, a number of popular authors blur purposes, and some of them do it exceptionally well. Bill Bryson, for instance, combines the purposes of informing readers about foreign places with that of entertaining. Other writers manage to write what almost seems like a reflection—which is written for personal reasons—designed to entertain an audience.

Because some authors combine purposes successfully, some English teachers believe that all students should do the same, even though the more successful of these writers are professionals: specialists who have developed their talents over many years and with a great deal of practice. Needless to say, most high school students haven't developed the skills to produce such stylized writing, so when teachers assign projects that call for multiple or unclear purposes, they tend to produce passionate pieces that convey more about their uninformed opinions than anything coherent.

Realistically, students do not need to learn to write like specialists who produce witty or sophisticated essays for a living; rather, students need to be able to communicate functionally to inform, explain, and persuade—without confusing or alienating their readers.

A DEVELOPMENTALLY APPROPRIATE ORDER OF WRITING PURPOSES

The more I confer with writing students, the more I see that writing is thinking on paper, and students who don't have ideas they want to write down have the hardest time generating writing. Students who are learning to write, more than anyone, need to be given writing tasks that match where they are at in terms of thinking ability. That is why I recommend assigning writing tasks in the order implied by Bloom's Taxonomy.

Bloom's Taxonomy is a model that describes the order of thinking skills from least to most complex. At the bottom is knowledge, which refers to rote memory and basic recall. After knowledge comes understanding, which implies not only the ability to recall or recite information but also to restate it in different words. Each level of Bloom's Taxonomy builds upon the level below it, so that a student who is able to analyze information will necessarily be able to use it, explain it, and recall it as well.

Higher-level cognitive skills

Evaluation

Synthesis

Analysis

Application

Comprehension

Knowledge

Lower-level cognitive skills

Many of the most common writing assignments align with the thinking activities described by Bloom, beginning with the second level, understanding. Students who understand what they are learning in their classes can organize their ideas and express them in informative essays that summarize, classify, or chronicle pieces of information in five-paragraph essays. These essays are the easiest to write in terms of thinking ability, and as such, they are the best types of essays to assign students who are learning to write essays for the first time or to apply a new set of objectives. A slightly more difficult type of essay to write will involve explaining concepts or ideas, while persuading an audience raises the level of challenge still further. Upper level thinking skills such as analyzing, synthesizing, and evaluating are, for the most part, postponed until students have had ample practice with simpler tasks. The most difficult essay that students will write in the basic composition course is that of comparison and contrast, which challenges students to analyze concepts.

Informative Essays

An informational essay requires students to provide a somewhat detailed answer to an academic prompt. Normally, students either generate three answers, or they generate one answer which they divide into three parts. These three answers (or three-part answers) become the three body paragraphs, which students develop by adding more details.

Informative essays can ask students to show understanding in specific ways. For instance, a classification essay asks students to organize information into categories and give examples that demonstrate how the categories work. Process essays ask students to show the order of stages and steps in a process. These essay types, along with familiar topics, tend to be easier for students to write than most others. Informative essays that require students to summarize abstract or complicated ideas are slightly more difficult.

For students who are still learning how to formulate an essay, prompts can elicit familiar information:

- Who are your heroes, or the people you admire most?
- What are your favorite Christmas memories?

Later on, your prompts will involve more academic information. Designing an academic prompt for a basic informative essay is not difficult: simply consider what aspect of what your student is learning you most want him or her to retain and formulate prompts that involve at least three potential answers.

- Who contributed to the development of the periodic table?
- What complaints did the colonists have against the British government?

Classification Essays

When introducing essay writing to students for the first time, the task of categorizing knowledge that is already familiar to the student works well. Not only do students feel comfortable with the content of the essay, the essay develops along a pattern that students should be able to apply to more complex topics later. Basically, prompts for classification essays ask students to generate three responses to an easy-to-answer question such as:

- What are the best kinds of books?
- What are your favorite kinds of music?
- What qualities make for the best friends?

The challenge in planning this essay is for students to make their initial answers—which become topic sentences when writing the essay—sufficiently abstract. Sometimes, students want to answer this kind of prompt with specific examples. For example, if a student answered the prompt "What are the best kinds of books?" with a response like "The Chronicles of Prydain series," he or she would have a hard time developing a paragraph that dealt with the question thoroughly; the specificity of the response gives the student nowhere to go except into a summary of Lloyd Alexander's books. Rather than a concrete example, topic sentences should identify broad categories or abstractions, so that a good topic sentence for the prompt above might say, "Some of the best books are fantasies." Then, students can name The Chronicles of Prydain in the paragraph as one of their examples.

Once your student has gotten the hang of writing a classification essay, you can formulate prompts that are more academic in nature:

- What are the main types of diseases? (Provide examples of each.)
- What types of plants flourish in our area—and why?
- What different types of governments do countries have?
- What types of inventions have most affected Western civilization?
- What qualities in various poems do you find most appealing—and why?

Process Essays

Process essays ask students to outline a process or sequence of events:

- How do you hunt caribou?
- How do legislators make laws?
- How may people prevent soil erosion?
- How does capitalism foster the development of new products?

With more concrete processes, as in the 'how do you hunt caribou' prompt, the task will be to organize the stages and describe the specific steps involved in carrying out the process in question. Students don't usually find process essays too difficult when the prompt elicits information about a concrete process with which they are already familiar. More abstract prompts, as in the 'how does capitalism foster development' one above, require students to outline an abstract process that they support with one or more specific examples, facilitating understanding on the part of their reader.

Summaries

Summarizing requires discipline to do well. In a summary, students do not merely repeat ideas verbatim but rather condense and restate information in their own words, showing that they really understand. Making decisions about what to include in a summary and how best to summarize an answer can be challenging. This is often true even for students who have found various creative writing assignments fun and easy in the past. And that's where it becomes clear that the student is entering a new stage in his or her academic career. Whereas writing creatively as many students do in elementary and middle school can be vague or sloppy, selecting precise words that convey information succinctly and accurately takes concentrated effort.

Choosing the right word can be challenging, but summarizing academic answers need not be daunting, especially since students can often find needed vocabulary in the texts they're reading. Many curriculums include review questions that require students to summarize information to show understanding. These prompts make it easy for you to assign writing that will reinforce what your student is attempting to learn.

For instance, the chapter review section of our biology textbook includes a number of short-answer questions such as "Describe how the different types of tissue work together in the skin, bones, and muscles" and "Identify five kinds of joints in the human skeleton. Describe the movement allowed by each joint, and give an example of each" (Johnson, 1998, p. 598). Prompts like these challenge students to summarize information. Many of these assignments call for no more than a paragraph response, and, since summary is all about concision, a well-written paragraph serves this purpose better than a rambling essay.

If the material your student is using doesn't include questions like these, you can write your own. Books that are not specifically intended as textbooks usually include helps such as tables of contents, lists of objectives, chapter summaries, or other features from which you can formulate appropriate prompts. For example, by flipping *The Everything American Government Book* open to the table of contents, I see that in Chapter 3, my student will read about the Bill of Rights: "How the Bill Was Born," "Freedom of Expression," "Protecting Rights," and more (Ragone, 2004, p. v). That information is more than sufficient to allow me to come up with several appropriate writing prompts, such as "What is the Bill of Rights, and how did it come into being?" or "What rights are protected by the Bill of Rights?"

Literary Summaries

Summarizing literary works challenges students to inform the reader of the contents of a book, but whereas summarizing academic information helps students crystallize knowledge they need to remember, summarizing literature serves less to help students memorize information as to understand how fiction works. Thus summarizing a literary work is a good exercise; still, requiring students to summarize or report on everything they read may inadvertently cause students to associate reading literature with work when in fact it should be a pleasurable activity. If reading and writing seem like chores to your student, I recommend you find prompts for most of your writing assignments elsewhere.

For students who enjoy reading, however, summarizing a book or writing a book review can afford good practice. It's actually a good idea to have students wait a while after reading a book to summarize it. Students who summarize a book too soon after reading it tend to ramble on about the bits they liked best, but after a while, they forget unimportant details and summarize only essential information about the setting and characters and focus most on the structure or plot of the work. This is how a book summary ideally should be: succinct and focused on the essentials. In this way, a student can summarize even a lengthy novel in a single statement such as this one:

> In Margaret Mitchell's classic novel, *Gone with the Wind,* a vain and high-spirited Southern Belle craves attention and security even as she confronts challenges during and after the Civil War, but while Scarlett O'Hara manages to provide for her family in the wake of her family's financial ruin, she never learns to be content.

Here is paragraph-long summary of another literary work which describes the plot in slightly more detail but, once again, captures the essence of the novel:

> In Daphne Du Maurier's classic novel Rebecca, the unnamed protagonist marries Mr. Maxim de Winter, a wealthy widower whose former wife Rebecca died in a tragic accident. The new Mrs. De Winter feels daunted when she hears stories about Rebecca's beauty, charm, and social grace from her new neighbors. She even begins to suspect that her husband compares her to his former wife and worry that maybe he thinks he has made a mistake in marrying her. Only when Rebecca's body is found drowned in the bay does the protagonist find out the truth about Rebecca.

For more about summarizing and writing about literature, see my book, *The Reader's Odyssey: An Individualized Literature Program for Homeschooling Middle and High School Students.*

Explanatory Essays

The next writing task requires students to explain. This task reflects a slightly more difficult level of critical thinking ability than that of merely informing because it asks students to infer why events occurred, to identify meaning behind actions or relationships between objects, or to provide support for personal positions. Whereas prompts that asked students to summarize information asked 'Who,' 'What,' and 'How,' prompts that elicit an explanation usually ask, 'Why?"

- Why do people eat at fast food restaurants?
- Why do various rocks appear so different?
- Why is exercise important?
- Why did the Populist party arise?
- Why did the South feel victory was certain before the Civil War?
- Why is inflation bad—or is it?

For some students, the slight increase in difficulty involved in explaining as opposed to informing will be almost imperceptible, and you will be able to assign academic writing prompts that call for students to either inform or explain almost immediately. For other students, the challenge of generating reasons may seem initially difficult. If this is the case with your student, don't worry. Remember that summarizing information develops critical thinking ability and keep providing your student with opportunities to practice. Eventually, your student will be ready to explain. In the meanwhile, try probing your student's readiness occasionally by assigning essay prompts that elicit explanation and talking him or her through planning the essay if explaining continues to seem difficult.

Persuasive Essays

A persuasive essay is essentially an explanatory essay that persuades readers to a particularly course of action or position. The planning process is nearly the same for this essay as with the last; the main difference is that whereas the thesis statement for an explanatory essay lists reasons for some phenomenon, here the thesis statement pushes a point and insists that somebody do something about it. A useful word in either the prompt or thesis statement for a persuasive essay is 'should.'

- Should high schools make volunteerism be mandatory for students in order to graduate? Why or why not?
- Should scientists use animals to test medications for humans? Why or why not?
- Should public libraries ban or restrict certain books?
- Should governments ration nonrenewable resources like gas and oil? Why or why not?

Notice that these prompts may or may not be tied to academic subjects. Although you can assign prompts like these and cater them to the subjects your student is studying, persuasive essays are often better when left to student choice. Students will feel more passionate and persuade more effectively if they're writing about a topic that they care about. Because persuasive essays should serve a real purpose, a good way to approach persuasive essays is to arrange for your student to present his or her essay to some group—ideally, a group of peers—as a speech.

Comparison and Contrast Essay

Still another type of essay calls for students to compare or contrast concepts, ideas, or literary works. This essay introduces a new purpose for writing: that of analyzing information. In contrast to purely informational essays in which students re-state information, a comparison and contrast essay involves more originality and discernment as well as a heightened need for organization.

The academic prompt for this essay challenges the student to first compare similarities and then contrast distinctions between two subjects—or vice versa. Students should attempt primarily one or the other, not both simultaneously. In order to organize an answer, students must first decide whether whatever they are writing about are more alike or dissimilar and then either focus on contrasting like items or comparing dissimilar ones.

For instance, take the prompt, "In what way were the experiences of immigrants recruited to work in Northern factories similar to those of slaves in the South?" Students should observe that the two groups are distinct and, in this case, the prompt even asks them to identify similarities; thus, their purpose is to compare the two dissimilar groups and draw a conclusion. On the other hand, when prompts call for students to find differences or distinctions between similar items, the purpose will be primarily finding aspects of the items to contrast. For instance, consider the prompt, "How were the suffragists of a hundred years ago different from the feminists of today?" Since both groups advocate women's rights, most people would consider the two similar. Thus, students must examine subtle distinctions between the two in order to draw an insightful conclusion. Of course, some comparison and contrast essay topics can be developed either way. Then, students must decide whether they will primarily compare similarities or contrast distinctions.

As before, prompts may be familiar or academic in nature:

- Compare and contrast a luxury car with a jalopy.
- Contrast and compare the exploits of Alexander the Great and Genghis Khan.
- Compare or contrast the Neolithic and Industrial Revolutions.
- Compare and contrast the original telephone to today's mobile communication.
- Compare and contrast capitalist, socialist, and communist economic systems.

The introduction of the compare and contrast essay is where students compare the objects they intend to contrast in the body of their essay or vice versa. For instance, the introduction paragraph below primarily compares models of phones, but the thesis statement reveals that the remainder of the essay will be primarily focused on contrast:

> **Everywhere you go these days, you see people talking on their phones. Since the invention of the first telephone, people have been able to dial a phone number in order to initiate a connection with a specific person and, once connected, talk into a receiver to communicate with the other person. In a way, not much has changed. Phones have always allowed people to communicate across great distances. Still, compared with the earliest models, today's phones have significantly better acoustics, mobility, and extra features.**

An insightful conclusion is what makes the compare and contrast essay analytic as opposed to merely informative. The body of the essay either compares or contrasts two topics and begs the questions, "So what?" and "Why does this matter?" These questions force students to generate a reasonable conclusion that moves beyond summarizing information to suggesting relevance. Responding to the question of relevance requires a higher level of critical thinking ability and lends substance to this essay's conclusion.

DESIGNING A SEMESTER-LONG COMPOSITION COURSE

How much writing should students complete in a given period? How much should you align academic prompts with what your student is studying? How do you make sure your student gets enough practice? Most programs provide a timeframe or at least a set of lessons so that you know when your student has ticked off course requirements. This one offers you only clear tasks and objectives. So how do you know what to assign and when?

My recommendation is that you form a plan at the beginning of each academic year to determine what types of academic prompts you will give, which subjects they will align with, how many products your students needs to complete, and how much freedom your student will have to opt for alternative activities.

Option 1: Align prompts with a single subject

This is probably the simplest composition plan: you combine the composition course with another academic subject and have the student write essays that reflect learning in the other subject. A natural candidate for this option is history. You may set a requirement for a specific quantity of essays your student will need to produce over the course of a semester or simply assign a new prompt whenever your student completes an essay. Either way, you can apply the content of essays toward your student's grade in the subject and the quality of the writing toward his or her grade in composition.

Option 2: Align prompts primarily with one subject and supplement with another

A second option aligns compositions primarily with one subject but allows room for some writing in another. For example, say an appropriate number of five-paragraph essays for your student over the course of a semester would be about fifteen. With this option, you might assign ten five-paragraph essays to your student over the course of a semester-long history course and reserve the equivalent of five essays for a second subject such as science, literature, or health. Compositions for the second course might also be five-paragraph essays done at intervals and interspersed with essay assignments for the primary course; alternatively, the secondary course might involve half-page summaries or short-answer paragraphs. This would be an attractive option if you wanted to document learning in more than one subject without overtaxing your student in either one.

Option 3: Alternate between academic and non-academic prompts

Another option is to design a semester-long course that calls for practice with several essays of each of the types described in this chapter. You might begin with a prompt that calls for a classification essay based on a familiar topic and then assign a more academic topic next and repeat this order with process, explanatory, and persuasive essays in turn. This option allows you to familiarize your student with all of the basic essay types so that you can assign prompts freely in the future.

For students who need more practice to feel comfortable with a task, you could pace this course so that new tasks are introduced only when students can independently plan and write the kind of essay they've been attempting. In that case, your plan would involve ordering the types of essays you'd like your student to attempt, but the specific number of assignments for each would be left open.

Option 4: Emphasize student choice by listing requirements

This final option may well be the best. Let your student choose how he or she will meet your requirements for this course. With this option, you must first decide what you need to see from your student over the course of the grading period (be it semester or year); next, you would identify three or four ways your student could fulfill those requirements. For instance, say I determined that my student could and should practice writing at least twelve five-paragraph essays per semester and that, of these, at least half should be academic in nature. I might then offer my student the following options:

- ☐ Write twelve five-paragraph essays in response to prompts about your U.S. history course in lieu of completing the end-of-chapter exercises and tests.

- ☐ Write six five-paragraph essays about your U.S. history course in lieu of completing the end-of-chapter exercises and tests; also, compose twelve half-page paragraphs: six literary summaries and six paragraphs about science.

- ☐ Write six five-paragraph essays about your U.S. history course in lieu of completing the end-of-chapter exercises; also, compose six five-paragraph essays on topics of your own choosing. For these, I expect you to attempt at least two different types of essay (informative, explanatory, persuasive, compare/contrast).

- ☐ Write six five-paragraph essays on topics of my choosing and six five-paragraph essays on topics of your choosing.

- ☐ Write six five-paragraph essays on topics of your choosing as well as twelve paragraphs (half-page minimum) in answer to my questions about literature, social studies, health, and science.

Allowing students to choose the option that appeals most to them can have a significant effect on compliance. High school students crave freedom, and most people want the freedom to think about ideas they find interesting. Since writing is thinking, students resent being made to write about topics they consider stupid or boring. Of course, high school students can rationalize that the reduced workload implied by the first option compensates for less than exhilarating topics. Sometimes, however, students cannot appreciate this compensation unless they choose it for themselves.

ALLOW STUDENTS TO SET THE PACE

Lots of opportunities to practice are what all students need. Don't feel like the goal here is to finish the course. The goal is not to finish but to develop skill. Don't rush this. Continue to give your student opportunities to practice with the types of prompts that elicit information, call for persuasion, or suggest comparison, and use these to challenge your student to develop the writing qualities described in the next few chapters. Do not proceed to the Advanced Compositions section until your student is consistently scoring around 90% on individualized rubrics you devise for clarity, coherence, and eloquence.

All students develop skills at their own pace. Some students will be ready to attempt advanced skills by their junior year of high school, while other students may not arrive at that level until senior year, and still others may not be ready for advanced compositions during high school at all. Especially for students who enjoy reading, writing ability can develop rapidly, but many students may need extra time to truly master each new quality. What matters is that students continue to make progress, however fast or slow.

Do make it a goal for your student to master the essential program. Every adult needs to be able to explain themselves, to analyze distinctions, and to persuade businesses and bureaucracies when necessary. The essential program described in Part 1 insists that every student learn to successfully write for all of these essential purposes. The advanced compositions described in Part 2 pertain primarily to skills that students will use in college. In fact, the advanced section covers skills taught in basic college writing courses. Students who progress to the Advanced Composition section can legitimately call their course "Advanced Composition" or even "College Composition" on their transcripts, and those who master that section's objectives should be able to test out of most Writing 101 courses.

Students who do not progress beyond the essential skills level but intend to attend college, however, are not behind. Many high school graduates today can't write clearly or coherently for any purpose, and they'll need to take remedial writing courses if they want to attend college, but students who learn the essential writing qualities described in the next three chapters will be well prepared for any situation life presents them, including college.

Chapter 6

Clear Content

A few years ago, I conducted a little experiment with my high school writing class. I gave my students three excerpts of non-fiction, and I asked them which excerpt best reflected the style of writing their essays should imitate. Two of the excerpts were clear and easy to understand—one, I believe, was from an essay written by E.B. White, author of *Charlotte's Web* and co-author of *The Elements of Style*, and the other was from Malcolm Gladwell's *The Tipping Point*. The third excerpt was from a sociology text entitled *The Homeless Mind* and contained sentences like, "The institutionalization of anti-institutionalism, however, by no means entails the demise of the latter as a theme in consciousness" (Berger, Berger, & Kellner, p. 213).

I did not expect my students to understand the highly abstract prose in the sociology excerpt; in fact, I included it specifically to make a point that, as it turned out, was not immediately obvious to my students. You see, in spite of having no idea what the excerpt meant, my students unanimously chose the sociology piece as the model they intended to emulate. Not because they understood the writing or found it clear, but because they assumed that the fact that they could not understand it meant that it had been written by someone smart.

True: the sociologists who wrote the scholarly piece of writing were smart, but they were also experts in their field—that's why their prose was so technical and abstract. Their writing reflected their thinking on specific matters. Unfortunately, a surprising number of high school students assume that their writing should seem smarter than they are. In fact, a piece of writing should seem only as smart as its writer. Students need to understand that high quality, intelligent-seeming writing is only high quality because it clearly reflects the good ideas of its author.

Clarity Occurs Through Revision

Clarity is an important quality of writing, but most students learn it not by drafting ideas, but by revising them. That is why you can expect the initial assessment of your student's writing, no matter how good a writer your student is, to be lacking in clarity. Writing is at least a two-step process: first, you get the ideas down on paper or out on the computer screen, and then you work to make them clear. Most students never take this second step but skip to the third, which is editing, or finding and fixing mistakes. Editing might fix superficial issues in a piece of writing, but revising for clarity exposes and resolves inherent weaknesses in the ideas themselves.

Initially, students will find revising for clarity difficult, but like everything else, with practice the process becomes easier: "Only after [students] have thoroughly assimilated these principles as habits of revision will they work their way into [students'] habits of drafting" (Williams, 2000, p. 53). Start teaching students the principles of clear writing early in their high school program, and by the time they graduate, they will have incorporated them into everything they write.

Three Issues that Affect Quality, Clear Content

Most unclear writing is not unintelligible but merely muddled, forcing readers to stop and re-read a sentence or paragraph in order to make sense of the writer's meaning. In fact, much of what impedes clarity in writing is not technically incorrect so much as symptomatic of writing that is less than perfectly clear. In my experience, three factors consistently lead to unclear writing. The first and most serious issue occurs when students attempt to write an essay without having any clear idea about what they are trying to say. That is why this chapter targets both clarity and content. Obviously, unless students know what they're trying to say, they cannot say it clearly.

The second and most common issue occurs when students fail to prioritize subjects, verbs, and direct objects as the main vehicles for conveying their ideas. Many students, even those considered to be good writers, compose unnecessarily convoluted sentences, conveying ideas that may initially seem impressive only vaguely. Often, sentences like these result from students having only a vague idea of what they were trying to convey. Because the students themselves have a general idea of their meaning, they assume their sentences are clear enough, but other readers find them confusing. Vaguely-written sentences may be grammatically correct and include remarkable vocabulary, but they also allow for multiple interpretations of what the writer meant; other times, they confound readers entirely. In contrast, a clear sentence expresses the writer's intended meaning unambiguously.

The third issue that crops up with many students is that they struggle with the rules of capitalization, spelling, punctuation, and grammar that make it easy for readers to understand what their sentences assert. Oddly enough, this is the issue that gets the most attention in school, but it is the easiest to mend. This chapter will help you address all three of these types of issues.

CONTENT THAT ANSWERS THE PROMPT THOROUGHLY

The first issue to address in any piece of writing is content. When students compose essays that express simplistic ideas or that attempt grandiose ones but don't support them, it is important to show students how to replace vacuous sentences and paragraphs with meaningful ones. If you feel like your student's essay is a little short or doesn't seem to say much of substance, read on. The next sections will help you see what your student's essays might be missing.

Strong Thesis Statement

When assessing whether a student has answered an academic prompt with sufficient clarity, the first thing to look for is a thesis statement that answers the prompt clearly. This thesis statement usually appears at the end of the introductory paragraph of a five-paragraph essay, although occasionally it occurs in the conclusion. A sound thesis statement holds the student's answer to the essay prompt, and the rest of the essay provides support for this statement in the details, examples, analogies, or explanations contained in the body paragraphs of the essay.

Most thesis statements will be a single sentence. For instance, if a prompt asks why the South lost the Civil War, you should be able to locate a sentence in the introduction paragraph that answers the question. For example:

The Confederate Army lost the Civil War because it lacked provisions, fresh troops, and ultimately, hope.

Do not confuse a thesis statement with an announcement of the writer's intent, which sets forth a general purpose for writing, but does not answer the academic prompt. For instance, for the same academic prompt as above, an announcement of intent might be:

In this essay, I will consider why the South lost the Civil War.

Students who use an announcement of intent to close the introductory paragraph should include a thesis statement in their conclusion.

Topic Sentences

Next, look for topic sentences. In a five-paragraph essay, the three body paragraphs should each begin with a topic sentence that transitions smoothly from the previous paragraph, links the paragraph to the essay topic, and specifies the purpose for each individual paragraph. Three topic sentences for the same prompt might be:

- **The South lost the Civil War because it lacked provisions.**

- **A second issue for the South involved diminishing troops.**

- **Ultimately, the Confederacy could not defeat the Union because it had lost hope.**

The thesis statement and the topic sentences together provide the framework for the essay as a whole. They also help the writer focus: without them, students tend to forget which point they're trying to make and sometimes fail to make any point at all. Topic sentences should be broad enough that students may develop sentences in support, yet clear enough that students can see what support the paragraph needs.

Supporting Details, Examples, and Explanations

Although a paragraph could develop any number of ways, the best support for any paragraph will answer the questions that will most likely occur to readers upon reading the topic sentence. For instance, upon reading that the South lost the Civil War because it lacked provisions, the reader wonders what provisions the South lacked and why the Southerners couldn't acquire them. Reading that diminishing troops caused the South's defeat makes readers wonder to what extent troops diminished, what caused the troops to diminish, and why the North didn't have the same problem. Similarly, reading that the Confederacy lost hope would make most readers wonder why.

To some extent, every paragraph will be unique and require a unique combination of supporting details, explanations, examples, and analogies. At the same time, different types of body paragraphs tend to follow certain patterns. For instance, because the Civil War example above is explanatory in nature, most of the support in body paragraphs would provide more detailed explanations. Other essay types also follow patterns that are somewhat predictable. The models provided in Appendix C can help students decide how to develop several types of paragraphs more fully.

Introductory Content

While most content occurs in the three body paragraphs, some basic information should be present in the introduction. Namely, the introduction of the essay should provide some basic context for the essay topic so that the reader knows what the essay is about, as well as any commentary needed to bridge the gap between the initial statement that introduced the general essay topic and the thesis statement for the paper as a whole.

Contrary to what many English teachers say, I don't consider a dynamite hook necessary in a five-paragraph essay. Not only are introductory hooks hard for immature writers to devise, they serve no authentic purpose in an academic essay. Hooks are rhetorical devices used by writers trying to convince an audience that what they have to say will be worth the effort of reading the rest of the article or essay. But realistically, the only audience for an academic essay is the teacher who assigned it, and frankly, teachers have no more option of not reading an apparently uninteresting essay than students have of not reading an apparently uninteresting textbook. At the basic five-paragraph essay level, any hook is icing on the cake.

Now, that is not to say that students should not add an appealing "hook" to their essay if one occurs to them, especially since more effective introductions do become necessary at the advanced writing level. Students at the five-paragraph essay level do well to include a simple hook such as a rhetorical question, a startling statistic, or a well-worded quotation. Otherwise, an adequate beginning to a five-paragraph essay simply starts with some point of common knowledge about the essay topic:

> **At the beginning of the Civil War, Southerners had every reason to believe that they would win. Not only did Southerners have more wealth and a strong belief in their cause, but the country's best and most experienced generals served their side. Indeed, at first, the Confederate Army won so many battles against the disorganized and ineffective Union Army that victory seemed eminent. Unfortunately for Southerners, most of those initial advantages did not last. In the end, the South lost the Civil War because it lacked provisions, fresh troops, and ultimately, hope.**

Conclusion Content

Many students mistakenly believe that the conclusion should repeat the main points of the essay. And, while it is true that a conclusion often reiterates, or touches upon, the essay's main points, a conclusion should never restate what has been stated in body paragraphs. In the body of a five-paragraph essay, students must stick to supporting a topic sentence without deviating from that purpose to include their personal opinions. But that does not mean that there is no place in a five-paragraph essay for personal observations: these are what go in the conclusion. In an academic essay, the conclusion is where students put their opinions about their topic, as in this opinionated conclusion:

> **Although initially the South had reason to believe victory was assured, ultimately, overconfidence led to ruin. In my opinion, though, the real culprits in the South were the political and religious leaders who encouraged people to believe fanatically in their cause. Most of what happened could have been predictable had people thought reasonably about what war would mean. Insufficient provisions and diminishing troops partially caused the South's defeat, but in the end, it was mainly the South's leaders who led their people into ruin.**

Another conclusion strategy suggests some kind of implication. With topics from history, this usually takes the form of suggesting how the lessons of history apply today:

> **Although initially the South had reason to believe victory was assured, ultimately, overconfidence led to ruin. As I consider our country's situation today, it seems to me that our country should not forget this lesson. In spite of economic uncertainty, our politicians keep committing American funds and troops overseas, assuming that our righteous cause, wealth, and power guarantee that we will prevail. But are we overconfident? The people in the South believed too fervently in their own cause, and they suffered a humiliating defeat. May our nation not make the same mistake today.**

Designing Goals for Improving Content

Express goals for developing paragraphs to convey adequate content positively. Try not to discourage inadequate paragraphs, as in "No paragraphs should be less than four sentences long," rather, state what students should do on future attempts:

Category & Criteria	Unacceptable; needs revision	Acceptable; meets the standard	Excellent; exceeds the standard
Body Paragraph Content	One or more body paragraphs lack either a topic sentence OR contain less than four supporting sentences	Each body paragraph includes a topic sentence and four supporting sentences	Each paragraph includes a topic sentence and four or more supporting sentences as necessary to adequately support the topic sentence

QUALITY SUBJECTS AND VERBS

Most students need focused practice writing with subjects and verbs. Do not skip this item, even if your student's writing seems relatively clear already. Not only is writing with subjects and verbs going to help your student write concisely and coherently, the challenge of picking the precise verb for each sentence will enhance his or her critical thinking abilities. Writing this clearly is hard, but students who discipline themselves to write with subjects and verbs eventually develop greater reasoning abilities, allowing them to convey increasingly complex ideas clearly and succinctly.

You may also be tempted to skip the focus on subjects and verbs if your student struggles much with conventions, and the glaring errors you see seem urgent. Trust me: spelling, punctuation, and grammar mistakes are never as serious as they seem. In fact, they are almost always fairly easy to fix. Developing good habits as a writer, however, takes time and practice, and furthermore, much of the confusion students feel about grammar and punctuation resolves once students learn to prioritize subjects and verbs. Teaching students to do so will actually fix many minor mistakes more effectively than focusing on those errors alone.

Understanding Subjects, Verbs, and Direct Objects

The clearest sentences convey meaning through the subject, verb, and direct object:

- **Mom bakes a cake.**

- **Researchers conduct experiments.**

- **The demonstrators demanded change.**

These sentences are clear. Because the sentences identify clear actors as subjects (Mom, researchers, and demonstrators), actions as verbs, (bake, conduct, and demand), and recipients of the action as direct objects (cake, experiments, and change), no questions remain. No one will say, "But what did the demonstrators want?"—the sentence makes it clear what they wanted. No one's going to say, "I don't understand. What are you saying about Mom in this sentence?" It's pretty clear what Mom's up to, and the people rejoice.

Obviously, these sentences are very simple, and most sentences are much more complex. But even in the longest, most complicated sentences, the greatest clarity comes from placing the meaningful words in the subject, verb, and direct object positions. True: sometimes experienced writers deviate from the clearest S-V-DO pattern in order to improve the flow of a paragraph, but when they do, these writers know why, and they compensate for the deviation to maintain clarity.

Sentences Patterns that Accompany Unclear Subjects and Verbs

Students who don't appreciate the importance of the S-V-DO combination for conveying essential meaning tend to write sentences that are either vacuous, pompous, or ambiguous in meaning. Some students write this way purposefully, because they think that writing for academic purposes means that they should flout their impressive vocabularies. This misguided idea probably comes in part from the fact that most vocabulary curriculums include more nouns formed from verbs than actual verbs, which tend to be shorter and more straightforward. As a result, many otherwise smart students write sentences that are wordy, pompous-sounding, or vaguely meaningful on first glance but ambiguous or confusing on closer inspection.

Other students simply don't understand how grammar works. This is especially true of students who have been exposed to one of the many language arts programs that advise them to make their sentences more clear by adding interesting adjectives and adverbs, which is a little like telling a teenager to put more stuff in his or her bedroom to enhance the visual interest. Listen: clarity demands less clutter, not more! Properly used, adjectives and adverbs hone meaning; they don't convey it. Students who have learned to write with lots of adjectives—and unfortunately, that seems to be the majority—need to understand how sentences are supposed to work.

If your student cannot identify subjects, verbs, and direct objects or use them appropriately in writing, I would advise you to take a break from composition and prioritize basic grammar. Though it may seem like a waste of time, trust me: taking the time to teach grammar can save years of frustration. One curriculum that I have found to be very clear and easy to follow is Genevieve Walberg Schaefer's *Understanding and Using Good Grammar*.

I have described two types of students who downplay subjects and verbs for different reasons, but in fact, almost every student who struggles with clarity employs one or more of six patterns that are more symptomatic of unclear writing than obviously wrong. Teaching students to avoid these patterns helps train students to prioritize subjects and verbs.

1. Expletive Construction

A sentence with an expletive construction usually begins, "There was" or "There were." Used appropriately, this construction shows existence:

There were ten marbles in my collection.

Most sentences use the expletive construction inappropriately:

There were many students that failed the test.

In this sentence, the expletive construction merely adds bulk; the real meaning appears in the adjectival relative clause. To revise the sentence, simply cross off the expletive, 'there were,' and the relative pronoun, 'that.' Revised, the sentence reads:

Many students failed the test.

Another expletive construction begins with 'it is' or 'it was,' in which 'it' refers to nothing specific:

It is significant to note that Smith has twelve marbles in his collection.

Because 'it' has no point of reference, the introductory clause is unnecessary: the only meaningful word in it is 'significant.' By converting that word into an introductory adverb, the sentence becomes more concise:

Significantly, Smith has twelve marbles in his collection.

2. Passive Voice

In a clear sentence, the subject does an action which the direct object receives: When Mom bakes a cake, the cake gets the baking. In a passive sentence, the subject receives the action of the verb, so that "The cake is baked." Sometimes Mom shows up at the back end of a prepositional phrase: "The cake is baked by Mom," but really, Mom's optional. We can leave her off if we like.

The problem with sentences in the passive voice is that readers like to know who is doing what, in that order. When I read "Mom bakes a cake," I picture first Mom, then Mom sticking something in an oven, and finally the cake. "The cake is baked" omits a crucial piece of information. "The cake is baked by Mom," gives me all the meaning but in the wrong order; it makes the cake more important than Mom. I don't care how much you like cake, that's just wrong. (She gave you life! Have some perspective!)

Of course, in a simple independent clause like this, clarity hardly suffers at all—no one really is confused about the cake—but in more complicated sentences, the passive voice can affect clarity significantly. Consider its effect on this compound-complex sentence:

Meetings are routinized to fixed times and places and the ceremonies in which [the village board members] participate are reduced to a pattern of talking which consumes time and accomplishes nothing. (Vidich & Bensman, 1968, p. 116)

The meaning here is less clear. Both verbs, 'routinized' and 'reduced,' are passive, and whoever is doing this routinizing and reducing is unnamed. It took me a few minutes to work out that this sentence is trying to say that the village board members meet regularly to waste time talking.

To convert a sentence from passive to active voice, apply the tense of the helping verb to the conjugation of the main verb. For instance, take the sentence:

A study was conducted to determine how people respond to stress.

The helping verb, 'was,' is in the past tense, so the main verb, which is 'conducted' needs to remain in the past tense. Now, take the passive sentence's subject and make it the direct object and ask, 'who or what conducted a study?" to find the subject. Sometimes, the subject can be located in the sentence with a phrase like, "by Martians" or something like that, but in this case, none exists, so you just have to do your best to come up with a reasonable answer. For instance:

Researchers conducted a study to determine how people respond to stress.

Simply tag the rest of the sentence on where it fits to complete the conversion.

3. Weak Verbs

Most people use weak verbs when they talk, so they tend to write with them as well. Weak verbs are verbs that can't get the job done by themselves; they need another word to complete their meaning. 'Make' is an excellent example because its meanings are so varied and so many common expressions use it. Consider its use in the following sentences:

- **The author makes his point clear.**

- **Andrew Carnegie made a lot of money by ripping off the workers in his steel mills.**

- **Franklin's role as ambassador made America's chances of defeating the British better.**

Though these sentences are acceptable, replacing the weak verbs improves concision and clarity in all three:

- **The author clarifies his point.**

- **Andrew Carnegie profited by underpaying workers in his steel mills.**

- **Franklin's role as ambassador improved America's chances against the British.**

Weak verbs tend to be common verbs that don't describe actions precisely without help. Try to picture, for example, the verbs 'take,' 'get,' or 'put:' without a context, the meaning is unclear. Whenever a verb in a sentence doesn't describe the literal action the subject is doing, suspect it of being weak. Sometimes, considering whether a verb literally describes the subject's action is all it takes for students to produce a better verb; other times, looking up the weak verb and its complement in a thesaurus supplies a stronger one.

4. Verbals Masquerade as Verbs.

Students who don't understand their parts of speech are often confused by verbals, which are words that look like verbs but act like something else. Verbals serve many purposes, as you will soon see; the difficulty arises when students think that a verbal is serving as a verb in their sentence or clause. Of course, since a verbal never serves as a verb, what results then is a fragment because every sentence needs a verb, and if you don't have a verb, you don't have a sentence. To show how verbals are supposed to work, let's go back to Mom and her baking.

In the sentence, "Mom bakes a cake," the verb is "bakes." To find the subject, you ask, "Who (or what) bakes?" The answer should be obvious, and it is: Mom. The direct object is similarly obvious: "Mom bakes (who or) what?" Mom bakes a cake. Easy. Next, consider three more sentences:

- **Mom wants to bake a cake.**

- **Mom hates baking cake.**

- **Mom, baking a cake, burned her thumb severely.**

In none of these sentences is 'bakes' the verb. In the first sentence, the verb is 'wants.' All that is happening here is Mom wanting. Cake is nothing but a gleam in Mom's eye; its future existence is hardly guaranteed. In the second sentence, "hates" is the verb. Mom hating is what's going on. Since what Mom's so busy hating is baking, cake seems unlikely, and you should probably stop drooling. In the third sentence, "burned" is the verb. Mom burning her thumb is the main point; "baking a cake" is an adjective that describes a simultaneous action. Thus cake is likely, but if you want some, you should probably express sincere regret and thank Mom for sacrificing her thumb on your behalf.

Here is the point: 'to bake,' 'baking,' and 'baking' were verbals in these sentences, and since verbals look like verbs but never work as verbs, students sometimes compose sentences that are in fact fragments; other times, students use verbals to compose unnecessarily wordy, mildly ambiguous sentences.

Infinitives like 'to bake,' 'to make,' 'to hesitate' or 'to undulate' are never verbs. Students often confuse infinitives with verbs and, as a result, include no verb in their sentence at all, making it a fragment. For instance, look at this intended sentence:

The pastry chef and her assistant to bake a hundred cupcakes.

Here, the writer clearly intended 'to bake' as a verb, but the sentence doesn't work. To correct this sentence, conjugate the verb, 'to bake':

The pastry chef and her assistant baked a hundred cupcakes.

Infinitives can also clutter up otherwise clear sentences. For whatever reason, many people conjugate verbs that don't actually describe what the subject is really doing in a sentence, as here:

The pastry chef and her assistant managed to bake a hundred cupcakes.

Although baking is clearly the main action in the sentence—I can't help but feel like the pastry chef and her assistant weren't primarily managing so much as baking here—functionally, "to bake" is acting like an adverb phrase, describing how or why the chef managed. It's a little less clear which, though, which is why this construction is slightly less clear than just stating that the chef baked the cupcakes and be done with it.

Gerunds look like verbs because of their -ing ending, but they act like nouns. Depending on where they fall in a sentence, words like 'baking,' 'making,' and 'fluctuating' can refer to conceptualized activities rather than actual actions. For instance, the gerund phrase, "baking a cake" conceptualizes an activity, as in:

Baking a cake is a glorious endeavor.

The only time a verb with an -ing ending is acting like a verb is when it follows a conjugation of the verb 'to be' or another verb that shows continuity:

Mom is baking a cake.

Mom keeps baking cakes.

Mom has been baking cakes since yesterday.

Mom will be baking cake until the cows come home.

In each of these sentences, 'baking' is the main verb, and baking is in progress. It's happening. Because progressive verbs look like gerunds, students sometimes confuse gerunds for verbs, although a reader usually has no difficulty identifying them as not-verbs because the sentence won't really make sense, as with:

Baking cakes as a hobby since she was a kid.

If your student confuses a gerund for a verb, simply explain that gerunds act like nouns as in the glorious endeavor of baking above, and advise your student to either add a subject and a helping verb:

Mom has been baking cakes as a hobby since she was a kid.

Or keep the gerund as the subject and add a verb:

Baking cakes has been Mom's hobby since she was a kid.

Participles and participial phrases are not verbs; they're adjectives. Students sometimes confuse a participial phrase for a complete sentence, as in:

Failing to recognize the suspect when he met him in the street.

To correct this error, simply attach an independent clause, ensuring that the subject refers to whomever or whatever the participial phrase describes:

Failing to recognize the suspect when he met him in the street, the detective missed his opportunity to arrest him.

5. Strings of Prepositional Phrases

This item specifically concerns strings of prepositional phrases, not prepositional phrases in general. Prepositional phrases are immensely useful; many if not most sentences contain at least one. What becomes problematic is when prepositional phrases contain most or all of the meaning in a sentence. For instance, in the sentence below, I've enclosed the prepositional phrases in parentheses and the adverbial phrase in brackets.

It is also an argument (for taking the variation) (in the periphery) (as a starting point) (for investigation) and, more importantly, (for examining the historical interaction) (of indigenous and foreign notions) (of political authority, structures (of domination) and mechanisms (of appropriation))) as they combine {to create the unprecedented circumstances and institutions (of politics) (in the modern periphery)}. (as cited in Lutz, 1989, p. 57)

Not only are the S-V-DO combinations lackluster, nearly all of the significant words appear as objects of prepositions. As best as I can make this out, I believe these 57 words mean something to the effect of:

I will examine the political interactions of indigenous people and foreign authorities, both in the past and now.

If your student composes sentences like the one above, you should probably take away your student's dictionary and refuse to give it back until he or she starts using plain English again like a normal person. But, more to the point, you have two options for sorting out a sentence that puts all the meaning into prepositional phrases. The first option is to ask your student to explain what the sentence means. If the answer is intelligible, advise your student to just write what he or she said.

If that doesn't work, ask your student to circle the three or maybe four words that are most important to the meaning of the sentence. Once your student has done that, ask which of the three the sentence is really about. That will be the sentence's subject. Sometimes, you will have to supply a missing subject, as in the sentence above. After I figured out that examining was what was happening, I had to guess who or what would probably be doing the examining. I chose 'I' because presumably, the examiner would have been the book's author.

Of the remaining words, one will probably be a nominalization, or a noun formed from a verb. Change that nominalization back to a verb; now you have a subject and verb. The third term will probably be the direct object, but even if it doesn't quite fit, your student should be able to clearly see what the sentence should have said.

6. Nominalizations Replace Verbs.

The preposition-heavy sentence above has many nominalizations: argument (argue), variation (vary), investigation (investigate), examining (examine), interaction (interact), domination (dominate), appropriation (appropriate). All of these words are nouns formed from verbs. According to English professor Joseph Williams (2000), more than any other choice a writer makes, using a lot of nominalizations "characterizes abstract, indirect, difficult academic and professional writing" (p. 49). Believing that they will sound more intelligent, many students with impressive vocabularies use nominalizations to beef up simple sentences. For instance, students write sentences like this:

> The absence of priorities and other pertinent data had the result of the preclusion of state office determinations as to the effectiveness of the committee's actions in targeting funds to the areas in greatest need of program assistance. (Lutz, p. 57)

Though impressive sounding, this sentence is hardly clear. Nominalizations obscure the sentence's meaning so that the reader has to piece it out, working backward from nominalizations to plain language. Clarifying a sentence like this is almost exactly like the process for sorting out the previous one: you look for the words with the most meaning in them and re-build from there.

In my reckoning of the sentence above, the nominalization 'preclusion' tells me that something kept the state office from doing something; 'determinations' tells me what it couldn't do; 'effectiveness' and 'actions in targeting' both reiterate that the office stunk at determining something specific. When I cut the junk, I get:

> **The state office couldn't determine which areas needed the assistance most because it lacked priorities and data.**

Improving S-V-DO Quality

Conveniently, about half of these—expletive construction, passive voice, and nominalizations—often rely on the verb 'to be.' Anytime you see that verb or one of its conjugations (am, are, is, was, were, be, being, been) as the main verb in one of your student's sentences, consider how it is being used. Chances are, it exemplifies one of the sentence patterns that reflect less-than-clearest quality.

These tics in isolation don't affect the quality of an entire essay very much, but the effect of many slightly unclear sentences throughout a paper accumulates. When a writer chooses awkward constructions often, the overall quality of clarity in the writing suffers. Therefore, if you spot one of these weaker sentence constructions two or more times in your student's sample essay, consider including the goal of replacing that pattern with a clear, *rubric* active S-V-DO combination on his or her individualized rubric, as here:

Category & Criteria	Unacceptable; needs revision	Acceptable; meets the standard	Excellent; exceeds the standard
Subject & Verb Quality	Verbs reflect the passive voice, as in "The cake is baked" in two or more sentences	Verbs reflect the active voice (Mom bakes cake), with no more than one passive sentence (The cake is baked) per essay	Verbs reflect the active voice consistently, as in "Mom bakes cake."

WRITING CONVENTIONS

Last and, yes, least important to clarity are writing conventions. Last, because many of the issues with punctuation and sentence structure ultimately boil down to not understanding the importance of subjects and verbs in sentences. Least, because word processing programs will detect many spelling and grammar errors even if students miss them. And yet, writing that contains errors in writing mechanics and conventions does need addressing.

Students who rarely make mistakes in writing conventions usually need only to have an error pointed out to them to see and correct it. If your student is one of these, flag inadvertent errors such as an extra comma or a missed word with a dash in the margin; your student should be able to easily see and fix the mistake. However, if your student persistently turns in papers with errors in spelling, punctuation, or grammar, you will need to decide if the errors reflect a lack of understanding that needs addressing or just sloppy proofreading. For the latter, you might want to institute a policy of not accepting papers that have three or more errors on them.

Students who don't understand how to correct errors need a different approach. These students feel confused and frustrated when teachers identify errors with cryptic remarks like "fragment" or "run-on" or "comma splice," and long lists of things to fix often overwhelm them. If your student is one of these, I recommend limiting the number conventions-related issues that you prioritize on the student's individualized rubric to the top two or three at any given time. Rubrics should explain the convention and, ideally, demonstrate a sentence that shows what the rule looks like. Then students become responsible for eliminating only the errors that pertain to the rules identified on the individualized rubric.

What about the other errors? You can either ignore them for the time being or write corrections on the paper for obvious errors like misspelled words or missing punctuation. That way, student can implement changes on the final draft without feeling overly pressured. Needless to say, errors that persist should be targeted on a future rubric.

A Few Common Errors

This section lists some of the most common errors students make, placing those that detract most from clarity toward the top and those that affect clarity somewhat less lower. For instance, the first few items involve capitalization and final punctuation, without which a reader cannot tell where sentences start and stop. Errors like these should be prioritized as objectives on an individualized rubric sooner rather than later; errors that appear further down the list can be addressed on subsequent rubrics in the order of gravity or appearance— that is, errors that occur most frequently in your student's writing.

This list is not comprehensive; it excludes a few issues, such as comma splices and dangling modifiers. Some of these will come up in later chapters. For instance, semi-colons and colons, which Lynn Truss calls "airs and graces" (p. 103), are addressed in Chapter 8. My object here is to help you prioritize those issues that specifically impede a reader's ability to understand a student's writing. For a more thorough resource, I recommend Diana Hacker's *Rules for Writers*.

Students should capitalize the first letter of the first word of a sentence, the pronoun, 'I', and proper nouns.

> Wrong: i grew up in minnesota, in dakota county.
>
> Right: I grew up in Minnesota, in Dakota County.

A complete sentence needs a subject and a verb and must convey a complete thought.

> Wrong: Baking a cake.
>
> Right: Mom bakes a cake.

Use a period at the end of a sentence; don't use exclamation marks in academic writing.

> Wrong: The demonstrators demanded change!
>
> Right: The demonstrators demanded change.

Use a question mark after a question but not after an indirect question.

> Wrong: Researchers wondered whether their conclusions were accurate?
>
> Right: Researchers wondered whether their conclusions were accurate.

Use an apostrophe to show possession.

> Wrong: Mom baked Bobs birthday cake.
>
> Right: Mom baked Bob's birthday cake.

Don't use apostrophes with plural nouns unless they possess something.

> Wrong: Mom bakes several cake's.

> Right: Several of the cakes' decorations were marred by the dog's licking.

Don't use an apostrophe with the possessive pronouns my, your, her, his, its, our, or their.

> Wrong: The dog earned it's scolding.

> Right: The dog earned its scolding.

Use commas in lists of three or more.

> Wrong: Mom bakes a cake, and a meatloaf.

> Right: Mom bakes a cake, a meatloaf, and a pot pie.

Use a comma before a coordinating conjunction when joining two sentences.[1]

> Wrong: Mom baked a cake but the dog licked off all the frosting.

> Right: Mom baked a cake, but the dog licked off all the frosting.

Use a comma to separate an introductory word, phrase, or clause from the main clause.

> Wrong: Sadly the dog licked the cake. (Makes it seem like the dog was sad.)

> Right: Sadly, the dog licked the cake. (It was sad that the cake was ruined.)

> Wrong: Seeing that the dog had licked the frosting Mom used the cake as a gift.

> Right: Seeing that the dog had licked the frosting, Mom used the cake as a gift.

> Wrong: Since the researchers learned nothing they didn't know how to proceed.

> Right: Since the researchers learned nothing, they didn't know how to proceed.

Use a comma between adjectives if you can replace it with the word 'and.' *

> Wrong: Mom bakes an appealing, delicious, carrot cake.

> Right: Mom bakes an appealing, delicious carrot cake.

Never put a comma between either the subject and verb or between the verb and direct object of a sentence (unless there is an interrupter—see next item for more about this).

> Wrong: Mom, bakes a cake.

> Also wrong: Mom bakes, a cake.

> Wrong again: The woman who lives in the hovel down the street, bakes a cake.

> Nope: My most excellent mother bakes, what appears to be a carrot cake.

> Right: The bakery that burned down last summer used to bake the best cakes ever.

---

[1] The most common coordinating conjunctions spell FANBOYS: for, and, nor, but, or, yet, so.

Use a set of commas to insert inessential or parenthetical information between the subject and verb or between the verb and direct object.

Wrong: Mom for all I know is baking a cake.

Right: Mom, for all I know, is baking a cake.

Wrong: Mom bakes among other things a cake.

Right: Mom bakes, among other things, a cake.

Do not use a set of commas if the information is essential to the sentence.

Wrong: The demonstrators, who vandalized town hall, were arrested.

(This suggests that all of the demonstrators vandalized town hall.)

Right: The demonstrators who vandalized town hall were arrested.

(Only the demonstrators who vandalized town hall were arrested.)

Any clause that begins with a subordinating conjunction needs an independent clause to complete it.

Wrong: When anyone has a birthday.

Right: When anyone has a birthday, Mom bakes a cake.

Pronouns should reflect the nouns they refer to.

Wrong: The group of demonstrators demanded change at the top of their lungs.

(The subject, 'group' is singular, the pronoun should be 'its.')

Right: The demonstrators demanded change at the top of their lungs.

Commas in Order of Importance and Difficulty

Type	Usage Tip	Example
List Comma	Use with three or more items, never with two compound elements	I went to the store to buy milk, bread, and cotton balls.
Introductory Comma	Marks the place where the independent clause begins	When the clerk started screaming, people looked at her.
FANBOYS Comma	Combines two complete sentences; the comma precedes the conjunction	I found the items, but the clerk was rude.
Terminal Comma	Use before a final added-on contrast element or question (right?)	Clerks should be polite, not rude.
Interrupter Comma	Use only with inessential or parenthetical material	Grocery stores, and all stores for that matter, should hire only polite clerks.
Replacement Comma	Use to stand in for implied words like 'and' and sometimes 'that'	Tomorrow I shall shop at the store with the nice, friendly clerk.

Generating the Rubric

So how does all of this translate into an individualized rubric that will target specific areas for growth? The three broad issues discussed in this chapter are ordered to help you prioritize goals. The first challenge for every student is to write essays with adequate content. That's why that item came first: students whose paragraphs lack development or whose essays don't answer prompts clearly need to work on those issues first. When content is no longer an issue, the rubric will prioritize objectives pertaining to writing with precise subjects and verbs; however, make sure the rubric retains at least one broad objective related to content. The reason for this is that no essay that fails to answer the prompt can be considered excellent or even adequate. In the same way, at least one objective should remind students about writing conventions, even if these are not an issue.

Treat conventions-related issues a little differently, especially if your student's needs turn out to be conventions-heavy. Students who struggle with conventions seem to master them more rapidly if fewer are targeted at any given time. Therefore, consider retaining the more complicated objectives on a rubric—such as developing content in body paragraphs adequately—over the course of a semester or year if necessary, while replacing mastered conventions objectives with problem ones on a quarterly basis and consolidating attained objectives into a single criterion moving forward. In this way, students may permanently resolve several conventions-related issues in their writing every semester.

The rubric thus serves two functions: it maintains quality control where no serious issues exist, and it targets areas for learning where problems emerge. In fact, when your student is ready to move on to the next chapter, which describes the quality of coherence, you will notice that the rubric for coherence requires students to write with clarity. That is because, of all the skills involved in writing, conveying clear content will take the longest for students to attain, and it is the most important for students to retain. Individualized rubrics can help your student achieve both.

Clear Content Rubric

Criteria	Unacceptable	Acceptable	Excellent
Content: Introduction	The writer provides no context for the essay's topic nor answers the academic prompt	The writer provides a context for the topic and announces an intent to explore the topic, but does not answer the academic prompt with a thesis statement	The writer provides a context for the essay topic, answers the academic prompt with a thesis statement, and provides an intriguing "hook" for the reader
Content: Body paragraphs	The writer omits a topic sentence, strays off topic in the paragraph, or develops less than four sentences that elaborate, exemplify, or further explain the topic sentence	The writer clarifies the paragraph purpose with a topic sentence and develops each paragraph with at least four sentences that elaborate, exemplify, or further explain the topic sentence	The writer transitions gracefully from the previous paragraph, clarifies purpose with a topic sentence, and develops four or more sentences that elaborate, exemplify, or further explain the topic sentence
Content: Conclusion	The writer repeats previously stated ideas, adding no new insights, evaluations, or recommendations	The writer reiterates the thesis (but does not repeat it verbatim) and suggests implications or adds an evaluation	The writer reiterates the thesis, offers an evaluation or suggests implications, and concludes with resonance
Clarity: Clear Subjects and Active Verbs	The writer conveys meaning through nominalizations, adjectives and adverbs; verbs are nondescript (i.e., have, make, do, be) or weak five or more times per page	The writer prefers to use clear subjects and active verbs but includes unnecessary weak or nondescript verbs, passive voice, or expletive construction 3 or more times per page	The writer prefers to write with clear subjects and active verbs and can justify any use of the passive voice or expletive construction; verbs are neither weak nor nondescript
Clarity: Complete Sentences	The writer does not break off sentences after conveying a complete idea OR the writer puts periods where commas should go	The writer brings sentences to a full stop with a period after the sentence's main idea has been conveyed	The writer constructs simple, compound, complex and compound-complex sentences correctly
Clarity: Conventions (Spelling, Capitalization and Punctuation)	The writing demonstrates more than 5 errors of any kind (spelling, capitalization, and punctuation) per page	The writing demonstrates no more than 3 errors of any kind (spelling, capitalization, and punctuation) per page	The writing demonstrates no more than 1 error of any kind (spelling, capitalization, and punctuation) per page

Clear Content Checklist

Essay Content

☐ Does the student introduce the topic of the essay?

☐ Does the student provide some kind of context for the essay topic?

☐ Does the student state a thesis or announce an intention?

☐ If the student announces an intention, is a thesis evident in the conclusion?

☐ Do topic sentences clarify each body paragraph's focus?

☐ Do the supporting sentences thoroughly answer the questions raised by the topic sentence?

☐ Does the student reiterate the main point of the essay in the conclusion?

☐ Does the student add a personal opinion or evaluation?

☐ Alternatively, does the student suggest an implication?

☐ Does the essay end conclusively?

Clear Subjects and Active Verbs

☐ Does the student avoid expletive constructions?

☐ Does the student avoid the passive voice?

☐ Does the student choose strong verbs and avoid weak ones?

☐ Does the student understand verbals and use them appropriately?

☐ Does the student avoid putting the most meaningful words in prepositional phrases?

☐ Does the student avoid inflating sentences with excessive nominalizations?

Writing Conventions

☐ Can the reader understand easily, unhindered by many errors?

☐ If not, is there a pattern of incorrect grammatical structures or punctuation?

☐ Is the pattern serious enough to be one of your top three priorities for revision?

Chapter 7

Coherent Progression

A well-written essay is like a jigsaw puzzle. Comprised of dozens, maybe hundreds of smaller pieces that fit together to form a complete and unified picture, a coherent essay draws a clear and reasonable picture with no major gaps, holes or misplaced pieces. If you have ever lost a puzzle piece, you know that even in a puzzle of 10,000 pieces, a single missing piece mars the effect—because, after all, mostly complete is still incomplete. Similarly, misplaced pieces have a disquieting effect: imagine a field of bright green winter wheat with a jigsaw-shaped piece of blue sky smack in the middle of it. The image wouldn't make sense; the misplaced piece would ruin the coherence of the entire picture.

So it is with essays that are poorly written. They don't complete a coherent picture, nor do their sentences fit together seamlessly. In an essay that lacks coherence, the disconcerting effect of logical jumps, gaps in the reasoning, and misplaced ideas build up so that readers lose confidence in the writer's argument. Even if the ideas are good, an essay that skips around and omits pieces will come off as unconvincing, if not irrational.

As you can see, coherence is essential. Having said that, however, don't try to teach coherence before students have a good handle on clarity. Coherence tends to elude writers who have not learned clarity, because they can't tell when their sentences are disordered, inconsistent, fragmented, or redundant. Students who don't prioritize subjects and verbs in their writing often ramble incoherently when asked to beef up their support. Only when students write clearly—more or less when their informative essays consistently score in the upper 80's or 90's on the Clear Content Rubric—will they be able to see how their ideas should be ordered for maximum coherence.

Three Issues that Affect Coherence

When your student is ready to tackle this new challenge, use the process described in Chapter 3 and the Coherent Progression Rubric provided on page 85 to generate a new individualized rubric. By now, your student will have generated plenty of essays, so you can either compare a few recent ones or assign a new prompt if you like. The best type of essay for this process will be comparison and contrast, which challenges students to organize their ideas somewhat more so than other essays.

Coherence is largely a matter of ordering ideas for the reader's benefit; it involves organizing the essay as a whole so that the main ideas progress in such a way as to make a point, organizing support to facilitate comprehension, and organizing each sentence to reveal each new idea to the reader as naturally as possible. A secondary aspect of coherence involves achieving the appropriate thoroughness in content, which means that the ideas neither overlap nor leave holes in the progression. As you may have already inferred, the items on the coherence checklist begin with issues that are easiest to discern and resolve and move toward increasingly difficult ones.

ORDER OF BODY PARAGRAPHS

You will remember that the thesis statement in a five-paragraph essay asserts the writer's three-part answer to the academic prompt, and that this answer aligns with the topic sentences and substance of each of the three body paragraphs. In a coherent essay, paragraphs retain the order of topics implied by the thesis statement. Ideally, this order will not seem haphazard: in the most effective essays, a writer thoughtfully orders ideas so that the points made reflect a logical or rhetorically effective progression.

In essays where this order is chronological, most students have no trouble ordering paragraphs. Chronological order is fairly obvious: a summary of historical events, for instance, will progress from the opening scenario to a conclusion in a straightforward manner, while a process analysis involves describing the stages and steps of a process in the order they occur. Normally, students have no trouble ordering these ideas chronologically.

It is when essays involve prioritizing assertions that students sometimes struggle. Many students fail to consider that the three ideas they generate to answer the essay prompt rarely achieve the same level of quality. Those that do pay attention to the uneven quality of supporting points often assume that they should prioritize their best ideas and subordinate their weakest ones. Unfortunately, when ideas in an essay progress from best to worst, the rhetorical effect on readers is poor: strong ideas impress readers at first, but then quality peters off, and they forget the initial strength and conclude that the essay as a whole is essentially weak.

Therefore, instruct students to order their paragraphs so that their strongest point appears last, where it will affect the reader's opinion of the essay most. The second-best idea should occur first, where it will intrigue and appeal to readers. Tell students to hide their weakest ideas in the middle, where readers notice mediocrity least.

Although attempting to determine the best order of ideas when drafting an essay makes sense, only after ideas are down on paper can students truly discern which paragraphs are strongest and weakest. An idea that seemed strong at first might fall flat once committed to paper; another idea that maybe seemed uncertain at first might gain clarity as it develops. Experienced writers make a point of considering the order of paragraphs early in the revision stage and improve this order if possible before making any other revisions.

ORDER OF SENTENCES WITHIN PARAGRAPHS

Once paragraphs have been sorted, look at the order of sentences within paragraphs to determine whether these represent a logically consistent progression of ideas. Most well-organized paragraphs primarily follow one of the four orders that people naturally understand: chronological, causal, analogical, and topical. Although paragraphs may be include more than one of these orders, generally speaking, paragraphs in an academic essay will prioritize one order to maintain coherence. Which of the four orders the writer follows pertains to the type of paragraph being written.

Perhaps the most inherently reasonable order is **chronological**. A chronologically ordered paragraph sequences events in support of an assertion made in the topic sentence. For instance, a paragraph with a topic sentence describing the near impeachment of Andrew Johnson might describe the sequence of events that led to that situation: first, Johnson kept vetoing bills and annoying many members of Congress; then, Congress designed a bill to ensnare Johnson and overrode Johnson's veto of it; subsequently, Johnson broke Congress's new law; finally, Congress put Johnson on trial to impeach him. The chronological order in such a paragraph clearly develops the sequence so that readers grasp how the assertion in the topic sentence came about.

A **causal** paragraph explains a cause or effect. For instance, a paragraph that sets out to explain why the Confederacy lacked provisions during the Civil War might list causes such as the Union blockade, decreased agricultural production, and Union confiscation and destruction of foodstuffs. Alternatively, the paragraph might select the most significant cause and develop it in greater detail.

An **analogical** order compares the topic of the paragraph and something that is generally dissimilar but alike in some particular way. The paragraph comparing a well-written essay to a jigsaw puzzle at the beginning of this chapter exemplifies this order. In such a paragraph, the topic sentence draws a comparison, and the paragraph's supporting sentences highlight similarities between the two items. A paragraph that develops an analogy should conclude by reiterating the analogical connection.

The final order, which is **topical,** is hardest to define because of its versatility. In an academic essay, a topical paragraph may categorize information, define concepts, support a generalization, or illustrate ideas about a topic.

Topical paragraphs that categorize or define follow a similar development in that both provide examples in support of either a definition or a description. Paragraphs that categorize information generally list multiple varieties of something, whereas a paragraph that defines concepts tends to provide one definition followed by multiple examples.

A topical paragraph that either supports a generalization or illustrates a position will name the generalization or idea in the topic sentence and support it with illustrative examples. For instance, a topic sentence that asserts the generalization that nineteenth-century immigrants were often stigmatized might be followed by examples of immigrants from different countries as well as some details about the stereotypes and stigma each faced. A topic sentence that asserts the position that dogs should be kept on leashes in public parks would be followed by illustrative examples that show various reasons why the position is true: even friendly dogs may frighten nervous children, dogs may get into fights, dogs poop, and so on.

In every case, however, a paragraph that follows a topical order must obviously stay "on-topic." However the paragraph is designed, every sentence in such a paragraph must be clearly relevant to the topic sentence.

In academic papers, the sentences in body paragraphs should serve a *primary purpose*: to sequence the events that led to the situation described in the topic sentence, to explain the concept or situation asserted in the topic sentence, to clarify an analogy, to define a concept, or to exemplify a generalization introduced in the topic sentence. Of course, it is acceptable for paragraphs to have both a primary and secondary order; however, paragraphs with both should retain a regular order of appearance. That is, if you were to convert a paragraph with two or more natural orders into an outline, the secondary order should apply to the same elements in the primary order with regularity.

When you and your student consider your student's essay, determine which order each body paragraph primarily reflects. Do the supporting sentences primarily reflect a natural order, or do sentences wander away from the paragraph's original purpose? For instance, the paragraph about Andrew Johnson was primarily chronological. If one sentence deviated from this order to explain why Johnson vetoed Congress's bill, this would probably be a good supporting detail for the paragraph, as long as the next sentence returned to the paragraph's primary purpose of chronicling the events. If the next sentence meandered off into more details about how bills are passed and why presidents have veto power, the paragraph would become confusing to readers.

As you can see, some deviation from this primary order is acceptable in a paragraph, such as to define a term or explain some important detail. There is a difference, however, between deviation (which implies returning to the task at hand) and meandering purposelessly. For the most part, sentences that don't reflect a paragraph's primary order or add useful information to its progression of ideas should be either eliminated, revised, or moved to another part of the essay where they fit better.

Once students know which natural order a paragraph represents, the best order for sentences to follow is usually apparent, and that is the beauty of natural orders: they are inherently reasonable. Once students understand that paragraphs must prioritize a single order in each paragraph, ordering sentences is rarely difficult.

ORDER AND THOROUGHNESS OF IDEAS

Somewhat more complicated is the matter of ordering ideas within or among sentences. Here is where the issues of omitted content, overlapping content, and discontinuous content arise, for even as faulty organization detracts from an essay's overall effectiveness, sentences that skip clarifying connections between ideas, sentences that restate what was previously conveyed, and sentences that start abruptly all reduce the coherence of an academic piece of writing. These issues are often harder to detect than out-of-order paragraphs or paragraphs lacking any organizing principle; still, a few patterns typify incoherence.

1. **Sentences begin abruptly.** This is often an issue in faulty topic sentences, where students sometimes start their sentences with the paragraph topic and conclude with the essay topic. For instance, in the Andrew Johnson example from above, a backwards topic sentence might say, "Belligerence on the part of Johnson is another reason Congress wanted to get rid of him." Even though the topic sentence as a whole might fit the paragraph that follows, the reader will feel initially as if the essay has strayed off-topic because 'belligerence' is a new concept in the essay which to that point had been generally about Johnson. Students often produce sentences that make their point backwards in this

way, beginning with a new idea that seems out of place to the reader and concluding with the connection to the previous point.

As you read your student's essay, watch for sentences in body paragraphs that begin with a term, a topic, or a subject that has not yet been introduced. Such sentences may actually be written backwards: that is, the term or topic that connects the sentence to previous ones may appear at the end of the sentence rather than at the beginning, where readers expect it. To resolve this issue, simply have the student identify the connecting idea as the subject of the sentence and have the sentence start there.

2. Sentences repeat the same ideas unnecessarily. This is where clear subjects and active verbs become imperative. Sentences that convey meaning vaguely—that is, through qualifying phrases and clauses rather than through subjects and verbs—tend to leave students feeling uncertain about whether they have communicated their points successfully. What often happens as a result is that they write multiple sentences to clarify a point, sometimes devising several that say more or less the same thing with slight variations. Then, having filled half a page with so much writing on a topic, students assume they have adequately supported the topic sentence and move on.

Conveying meaning through subjects and verbs eliminates this potential pitfall. When the meaning in a sentence is perfectly clear, students never communicate the same idea twice because the subjects and verbs will either look exactly the same or be synonymous. This is why experienced writers revise sentences for clarity before they revise for coherence: clarifying sentences often reveals redundant ideas. Two sentences with the same subject and verb, even if they assert two slightly different points through distinct direct objects, can easily be combined. The resulting compound sentence will eliminate unnecessary wordiness or redundancies.

Sometimes, a writer will write essentially the same sentence—that is, same subject, verb, and direct object—twice, in two different paragraphs. This is another form of redundancy that sometimes occurs, usually when a student is confused about how to organize his or her ideas. When this happens, it's good to sketch an outline of the essay's ideas on a separate piece of paper and have the student decide where the idea truly belongs. Then, to revise the essay, have the student move the redundant text next to the similar sentence and compare them. The student can then pick the sentence that best conveys the idea or, if appropriate, blend the two sentences so that the nuances of each are retained. The resulting sentence should be stronger than either of the two redundant ones.

3. Sentences skip subtle connections. This item refers to the phrases and clauses that complete ideas, rather than obvious holes in the natural order which discerning the paragraph's organizing principle will have revealed. Unless the writer interrupts a progression to clarify a parenthetical point, supporting sentences should begin with an idea that has already been introduced and move to a new idea or concept. This movement from old to new is what I call the paragraph's progression of ideas: each sentence moves the progression forward. Sometimes, however, students unconsciously assume readers know a piece of information that they feel is obvious and exclude it, leaving a gap in their progression.

One way to detect gaps like these is by considering whether the subject in each sentence was introduced in the previous sentence. Concepts should pick up where the last sentence ended, like tiles in a game of dominoes that must match up the markings on the last played piece. Does the subject for the sentence appear—not necessarily verbatim, but conceptually—in the previous sentence? Alternatively, does the conclusion of the previous sentence lead the reader directly to the subject concept? If not, the sentence should be revised or another sentence inserted so that the last logically important idea connects to either the next idea or to the paragraph's topic.

Gaps Students Often Leave

One of the most common omissions is failing to use **transitions** to show how ideas relate to one another. In terms of coherence, transitions are especially important when ideas switch gears or contexts. In this paragraph, missing transitions detract from the paragraph's coherence:

> **The first modern toothpastes appeared on the market for general consumption. They consisted of a blend of hydrogen peroxide and baking soda and were packaged in collapsible tubes made of lead. Fluoride was added to some toothpastes, but the American Dental Association disapproved. The benefits of fluoride for reducing tooth decay became widely accepted and fluoride toothpaste became popular.**

The paragraph makes more sense with transitional phrases:

> **Around the late 1800's, the first modern toothpastes appeared on the market for general consumption. At that time, the toothpaste consisted of a blend of hydrogen peroxide and baking soda and was packaged in collapsible tubes made of lead. Later, fluoride was added to some toothpastes, but the American Dental**

Association disapproved of the addition. After World War II, the benefits of fluoride for reducing tooth decay became widely accepted, but not until the 1970's did fluoride toothpaste become popular.

Another typical omission is the failure to provide **concrete examples for generalizations**. For instance, a student might write something like this:

The conquistadores treated the indigenous peoples barbarously. They were cruel to the native peoples because they did not consider them entirely human.

What's missing? Details—and proof. Where's the support for the assertion that the conquistadores treated people barbarously? The writing omits concrete examples that illustrate the barbarous treatment:

The conquistadores treated the indigenous peoples barbarously. In Hispaniola, they burned the native chief Hatuey alive. They used their advanced weaponry to massacre native peoples and intimidate survivors into working in silver mines. In South America, conquistadores used specially trained dogs to disembowel the native peoples. They then forced indigenous people to work in silver mines, where many died due to the brutal labor and mercury poisoning. The conquistadores were cruel and treated indigenous peoples inhumanely.

Similarly, students often fail to provide **concrete examples for abstract concepts**:

The Common Law prohibited encroachment. Encroachment is defined as crossing beyond proper limits. Under the Common Law, someone who committed encroachment had to make restitution or be considered an outlaw.

Here, the writer defines 'encroachment,' but without concrete examples, the reader may struggle to visualize the concept. A few examples clarify the concept:

The Common Law prohibited encroachment, which may be defined as crossing beyond proper limits. For example, a farmer who let his cattle graze on someone else's property would be encroaching. More extreme forms of encroachment would be stealing someone else's property or attacking and injuring another person. Under the Common Law, someone who committed encroachment had to make restitution or be considered an outlaw.

Students often forget to spell out both parts of a statement that shows **contrast**:

In 1900, women in most states were not allowed to vote, run for office, or enlist in the military. Today, all of those things have changed.

Here, exactly what change the student is pointing to is unclear. The reader would understand better if the student included the rest of this contrast:

> In 1900, women in most states were not allowed to vote, run for office, or enlist in the military, but gradually women began to challenge these limitations. In 1916, Wyoming residents elected Jeanette Rankin to serve in Congress, and in 1920, the 19th Amendment gave women the right to vote. In 1942, the Women's Army Corps expanded opportunities for women, who had previously been confined to the role of nurse only. Today, women can do all of the things that were prohibited one hundred years ago.

Another issue for many students is providing **partial explanations**. This tends to occur when students explain a chain of events and leave out one of the links:

> Scientists think that the earth's climate is getting warmer. They believe that the reason for the earth's rising temperature has to do with burning fossil fuels to power factories, heat homes, and run cars.

These sentences are not incorrect, but they skip a crucial connection: how and why do fossil fuels make the earth hotter? Explanations need to answer reader's questions as they arise, so students need to answer how or why with each sentence:

> Scientists think that the earth's climate is getting warmer. They believe that the reason for the earth's rising temperature has to do with increasing levels of carbon dioxide in the atmosphere. This carbon dioxide comes from burning fossil fuels, which consist mainly of carbon, to power factories, heat homes, and run cars.

Finally, students need to watch out for **weak analogies**. Analogies are weak when they fail to make the pertinent connections clear for readers:

> When the confederated states failed to honor their promises, they fell into chaos and disorder, just like when Eve ate the apple. Because of Eve's Fall, God made her subject to Adam. So it was with the Articles of Confederation.

Students often fail to realize that analogies are highly individual: when they occur to us, they seem perfectly reasonable (and usually quite brilliant)—and they might well be reasonable (and brilliant)—but usually, other people cannot understand them unless a writer explains specifically how the analogy fits the topic. The analogy above, for instance, needs to show how both Eve and the states under the Article of Confederation 'failed to honor,' and were subsequently 'subjected' to a more powerful force:

When the confederated states failed to honor their promises, they fell into chaos and disorder, just like when Eve ate the apple. Because Eve dishonored her promise not to eat from the Tree of Knowledge, selfishness and discord entered the world, and God had to intervene to restore order. He made Adam ruler over Eve and gave him more power so that she had to obey him. In the same way, when the states failed to honor the Articles of the Confederation, the Founding Fathers drafted a new Constitution that each of state in the Union would be forced by a powerful national army to obey.

Generating the Rubric

As you consider your student's sample essay(s), ask where the student's ordering of paragraphs, sentences, and ideas within sentences strike you as slightly off. Do the paragraphs diminish in effectiveness, leaving you less convinced at the end than at some previous part of the essay? Do the sentences within paragraphs follow a natural order that seems inherently reasonable? Do the ideas flow neatly from one concept to the next, with no redundancies and no logical gaps? Use this information to determine which coherence issues most affect your student's writing.

Note that issues of coherence often affect students more as the writing reflects higher critical thinking skills. Therefore, once your student advances to writing essays with both clarity and coherence, challenge your student to write more essays that persuade and analyze and fewer that call for summarizing information only. Coherence may also suffer when writing tasks become more expansive. Organizing research papers or arguments sometimes fluster students who previously did not struggle with coherence. For such assignments, students do well to organize the paper by sections first, and then order paragraphs within each section. More information about organizing information in lengthy compositions can be found in Chapter 9.

Also, you will notice that the Coherent Progression Rubric on the opposite page retains three criteria from the previous chapter. I would recommend that you either keep these three broad objectives on the rubric you design for teaching coherence or, if your student still has a few specific tics pertaining to clarity, to target specifically those—but certainly, keep the broader purpose of writing with clarity in mind as you and your student evaluate essays for coherence.

Coherent Progression Rubric

Criteria	Unacceptable	Acceptable	Excellent
Content: Thesis statement and essay as a whole	The writer does not answer the academic prompt in the thesis statement or topic sentences	The writer clearly answers the academic prompt with a thesis statement and develops three body paragraphs with topic sentences supported by details and examples	The writer answers the academic prompt in the thesis statement, develops three body paragraphs with topic sentences supported by details and examples, and concludes by suggesting implications or an evaluation
Clarity: Subjects and Verbs	The writer conveys meaning through nominalizations, adjectives and adverbs; verbs are nondescript (i.e., have, make, do, get, be) or weak in five or more sentences per page	The writer prefers the use of clear subjects and active verbs but includes up to three sentences per page with unnecessary expletive construction, passive voice, or weak or nondescript verbs	The writer prefers to write with clear subjects and active verbs and can justify any use of the passive voice or expletive construction; no verbs are weak or nondescript
Clarity: Sentence correctness	Sentences run on or are incomplete; they demonstrate more than 5 errors (spelling, capitalization, and punctuation) per page	Sentences are complete and demonstrate no more than 3 errors of any kind (spelling, capitalization, and punctuation) per page	Sentences are complete and demonstrate no more than 1 error of any kind (spelling, capitalization, and punctuation) per page
Coherence: Paragraph order	Paragraphs follow no particular order OR paragraphs decrease in strength of ideas	Paragraphs follow a logical order	Paragraphs increase in strength so that the strongest paragraph is last and the weakest paragraph comes second
Coherence: Sentence order	Body paragraphs do not reflect any primary order of development; some sentences appear to be out-of-order or off-topic	Supporting sentences in body paragraphs reflect a single primary order (causal, chronological, topical, or analogical) and occur in a logically appropriate order	Sentences in body paragraphs reflect a single primary order (causal, chronological, topical, or analogical), and occur in a logically appropriate order; any interruption to this order provides necessary clarification
Coherence: Thorough support for all points and sub-points	Some sentences initiate with new ideas or concepts; some sentences restate previously established ideas or leave out necessary connections	Each sentence initiates with previously introduced ideas and establishes new ideas; any gap or overlap is very slight	Each sentence initiates with previously introduced ideas and establishes new ideas; no gap or overlap is evident

Coherent Progression Checklist

Paragraph Order

☐ Do the paragraphs follow the order implied by the thesis statement?

☐ Do the paragraphs follow a natural order? OR

☐ Does the student conclude with his or her strongest paragraph?

Sentence Order

☐ Do the sentences follow a natural order?

☐ If the paragraph includes two or more natural orders, can you tell which is primary?

☐ Do secondary order sentences follow primary-order sentences with regularity?

Order and Thoroughness of Ideas

☐ Do sentences begin with familiar terms and concepts?

☐ Do sentences avoid repeating ideas, either verbatim or synonymously?

☐ Do transitions indicate changing directions or contexts?

☐ Do students provide concrete examples for generalizations?

☐ Do concrete examples give definition to abstract ideas?

☐ Does the student develop both ideas when showing contrast?

☐ Does the student answer how or why for each part of his or her explanations?

☐ Does the student connect each pertinent aspect of analogies to assertions?

Chapter 8

Eloquent Prose

If coherence can be compared to a jigsaw puzzle, eloquence is like a figure skating routine. Either the elements flow smoothly and occasionally wow spectators, or they seem pieced together and shaky, and occasionally they fall apart. In skating, most people notice only the obvious: landed jumps versus falls, graceful spins versus wobbly ones. Although commentators talk about edges and rotations and whatnot, the average person can't tell what skaters do to make routines spectacular versus just okay. In the same way, what makes prose eloquent versus just correct is subtle: most readers don't know how writers achieve eloquence, but they know and appreciate it when they see it.

Eloquence in an academic essay involves conveying clear and coherent, easy-to-follow ideas with a pleasing rhythm that some people call style. Of course, some of the most eloquent writers, poets, and novelists, express their ideas eloquently but not clearly or especially coherently, and that is because ambiguity is desirable in those kinds of writing. But in an academic composition, content must remain clear and coherent. Think about it: an academic essay that is eloquent yet incoherent is qualitatively worse than one that is coherent but lacking in eloquence. Therefore, retain objectives for clarity and coherence in individualized rubrics as students learn how to apply this new quality to their writing.

Three Issues that Affect Eloquence

Introduce eloquence after your student has demonstrated a grasp of the principles of writing coherently, but since many writers find it convenient to revise for both simultaneously, mastery of coherence is not as much of a prerequisite here as mastery of clarity was for learning coherence. Still, students benefit from dedicating time to learning what coherence is and how to recognize signs of incoherence in their own writing before learning to apply the principles of eloquence, which are more subtle and somewhat less important to the overall effect of a piece of writing. I recommend introducing this quality when students are scoring in the 80's range on coherence objectives. Students should have a good sense of how to revise essays to improve coherence before considering eloquence as well. As before, follow the steps described in Chapter 3 to generate an individualized rubric and use the rubric for eloquence found on page 97 to assess your student's initial essays. As you identify specific goals for your student at this stage, focus on the following three issues.

PARALLEL IDEAS WITHIN SENTENCES

The first issue affecting eloquence involves symmetry and balance. When sentences convey grammatically equivalent ideas in the same grammatical way, what results is a parallel structure that readers find rhetorically pleasing and logically satisfying. When a sentence conveys ideas that are logically equivalent with different grammatical structures, the effect can be slightly jarring:

I like to run, bike, and go skiing.

The sentence rhythm is off because the three activities should be equal, but the aberration in grammatical structure lends an unnatural primacy to the last item. This sentence is better:

I like to run, bike, and ski.

Parallel structures group grammatically equivalent ideas with coordinating conjunctions such as 'and,' 'but,' 'or' and 'nor.' Coordinating conjunctions allow writers to tightly combine parallel subjects, verbs, direct objects, phrases, clauses—almost any grammatical function or structure can be combined neatly and in such a way that readers easily understand and appreciate. Most students will be familiar with the concept of compound subjects, verbs, and direct objects, which are often taught in grade school:

- **Mom and Suzie bake cake.**

- **The ladies bake and eat cake.**

- **The ladies bake muffins, cookies, and cake.**

Simple compound functions in simple sentences like these seem almost simplistic. And, certainly, a paragraph of simple sentences like these would be. But consider the effect of compounds reflecting a variety of grammatical functions and structures:

Tocqueville observes that, while an obscure journalist's opinion has almost no influence, an opinion held by many journalists has an "almost irresistible" influence over society (178). Anyone who dares express an opinion contrary to the popular view exposes himself to a kind of exile: those who disagree with the dissenter openly condemn not only his view but often his very person, while those who agree usually lack the dissenter's courage and say nothing.

Not so simplistic, is it? Using compound elements to sound sophisticated is all about balance and precision. This excerpt balances several grammatically equivalent ideas:

- **an obscure journalist's opinion has almost no influence [while] an opinion held by many journalists has an "almost irresistible" influence**

- **those who disagree with the dissenter [versus] those who agree**

- **openly condemn [while others] usually lack**

- **not only his view [but] his very person**

- **lack . . . courage [and] say nothing**

Parallel structures do two things for prose. First, parallel grammatical structures achieve a pleasing, natural rhythm, as in the sentences above. Second, parallel grammatical forms convey clear ideas as concisely as possible, often reducing the word count of complicated sentences significantly. Thus parallel structures help students combine sentences economically and gracefully. By combining sentences that share grammatically equivalent ideas with parallel structures, students retain all of their meaning, improve the coherence of their paragraph, and impress the reader with their masterful writing style.

Punctuating Parallel Structures

Using parallel structures well challenges students to use semi-colons and colons, both of which serve list functions. All compound elements are essentially lists, sometimes of just two compound elements, sometimes more. Incidentally, two compound elements don't require commas, even if they're long, as with relative clauses or verbal phrases. The only exception here is when the two compound ideas are independent clauses, which may be combined with a coordinating conjunction plus a comma, or without the coordinating conjunction and with a semi-colon or a colon. Since most students will not have used these punctuation marks extensively before now, it may be a good idea to consider how colons and semi-colons work in parallel structures.

Colons

The list-function colon appears after a complete sentence, after which a list of appositives name whatever was abstractly identified in the sentence:

> **Before going to the store, Santa made a list of the items he would need this year: air sickness tablets for the journey, pepper spray for rambunctious pets, Airborne to ward off viruses, and a case of energy drinks to keep him from dozing off again over Nebraska.**

Notice that the colon follows a complete sentence, and the list that follows the colon names the referred to 'items'.

Another colon use has a similar function: it explains a vague idea conveyed in the first of two independent clauses. An example of this is found in the sentence from above:

> **Anyone who dares express an opinion contrary to the popular view therefore exposes himself to a kind of exile: those who disagree with the dissenter openly condemn not only his view but often his very person, while those who agree usually lack the dissenter's courage and say nothing.**

Before the reader says, "What do you mean, 'a kind of exile'?" the second half of the sentence is answering that question with a more detailed explanation. I call this the "ta-dah!" colon because it says, "ta-dah!—here's what I mean" before the reader has a chance to process the idea that the first clause wasn't entirely clear. These colons enable a parallel construction wherein a clause asserts something that a second clause makes clear.

Semi-Colons

Similarly, semi-colons combine closely related independent clauses:

> **People in a democracy habitually adopt popular ideas; they rarely engage in serious thought.**

When you combine two independent clauses—such as the ones above—with a comma rather than a semi-colon, zealous English teachers suffer small fits and write 'comma splice' in the margins of the paper. Students are often confused by the whole comma splice thing, since many popular authors use them frequently (in fact, the book I am reading now—a bestseller—is full of them). Still, using semi-colons correctly gives one a certain sense of accomplishment that makes young writers feel almost giddy with power—or, as in Lynn

Truss's letter to her eighth grade American pen-pal (who had written to her in "huge handwriting, like an infant's"), condescension:

> In my mission to blast little Kerry-Anne out of the water, I pulled out (literally) all the stops: I used a semicolon. "I watch television in a desultory kind of way; I find there is not much on," I wrote. And it felt so good, you know. It felt fantastic. It was like that bit in *Crocodile Dundee* when our rugged hero scoffs at the switchblade of his would-be mugger, and produces a foot-long weapon of his own, "Call that a knife? THAT's a KNIFE." (p. 104-105)

(Not to fear, the attitude is not an essential feature of semi-colon usage.)

Like colons, the semi-colon also has a list-function: it separates groups in lists containing commas—in which case, the semi-colon is sort of like a super-comma:

> **Santa delivers classic toys like dolls, balls, and tops; educational toys like electronic spelling games, math flash cards, and talking globes; and trendy toys like iPods, Xboxes, and Wiis.**

SENTENCE RHYTHM

The second issue with eloquence involves rhythm, and the only way to deal with it is by revising sentences with flawed rhythm that seem stilted or droning or otherwise awkward. Although people usually associate rhythm with sound, in fact you can sense the rhythm of words in sentences and in paragraphs; generally, however, no one really notices rhythm in writing unless it's flawed.

One way to improve the rhythm of a sentence is to use parallel structures, as with the "I like to run, bike, and ski" example above. Another way to improve flawed rhythm is to make sure that sentences are not all starting the same way or repeating the same basic sentence patterns. For instance, a paragraph containing only simple sentences will feel stilted and monotonous in a Dick-and-Jane sort of way:

> **Short sentences bore readers. Readers dislike monotony. The rhythm feels wrong. This paragraph doesn't flow. These sentences seem simplistic.**

If simple sentences seem choppy, paragraphs of solely compound-complex sentences, even when carefully crafted with parallel structures, seem tedious:

High school students usually avoid writing strings of short sentences because they understand that short sentences pertain to younger students and because they want to seem and sound more educated and sophisticated. Compound-complex sentences certainly reflect greater complexity of thought and a higher level of education, yet writers who employ them exclusively give readers the impression of a lecturer who fails to consider the needs of the audience for more pleasing rhythms. It does not matter if the content of the sentences is clear and coherent nor if the topic is inherently intriguing because the constant drone and lack of rhythm gradually lulls listeners and puts them to sleep. A more pleasing rhythm results when the writer employs various sentence types and especially when the writer begins sentences with different introductory methods. These sentences all begin with subjects and verbs, and they all seem monotonous and dreary as a result.

Painful, wasn't it? And yet, I hope I have made my point: a pleasing rhythm results from varying the type, length, and introductions of sentences. Many high school students wrongly assume that they should never compose short sentences. In fact, a single short, snappy sentence breaks up the monotony of a string of compound or compound-complex sentences, improving the paragraph's rhythm dramatically.

Another issue that affects rhythm is repetitive sentence structures, especially in the way sentences begin. Generally speaking, the rhythm of a paragraph suffers if even two sentences repeat the same exact structure. Beginning consecutive sentences with an introductory word or phrase, for instance, sounds awkward:

> **Actually, I like introductory words. Consequently, these sentences sound repetitive. Frankly, this paragraph needs revising. Happily, that won't be hard.**

Did you feel the choppy rhythm? The good news is that knowing about writing tics like these helps writers remember to watch for them and revise accordingly. For instance, when I find that I have written two or more consecutive sentences with the same structure, I simply move a phrase to a different part of the sentence or I combine my sentences differently. Either one adjusts the paragraph's rhythm. Here's the same awkward paragraph from above, revised:

> **I like introductory words, but using them too consecutively sounds repetitive. Happily, revising this paragraph wasn't hard at all—I just eliminated all but one of the introductory words.**

APPROPRIATE EMPHASIS

The third item that affects eloquence in a paragraph is appropriate emphasis. In a well-designed paragraph, the ideas that the writer wants readers to recall should receive emphasis and resonate, or linger, with the reader. Of course, the idea that should resonate most in any essay will be the writer's conclusion. Thus writing with appropriate emphasis involves ordering ideas so that sentences and paragraphs lead to the ideas that the writer wants to emphasize. In other words, the point that the writer is trying to make should come last in both sentences and paragraphs.

This is very similar to one of the items students learned regarding coherence: the ideas in a sentence and the sentences in a paragraph should move from previously introduced material toward new material. This is how coherent essays work: they gradually move from some point of general knowledge toward a specific, new idea that the writer wants the reader to note and remember. When the prose is eloquent as well as coherent, the writer's main idea will not only seem logical, it will feel substantial and conclusive as well.

This emphatic, conclusive feeling can be attained in two ways. The first way is to conclude with a short, punchy wrap-up sentence. This strategy works best when the writer's conclusion consists of a single assertion and follows a series of fairly complicated sentences. This goes back to the idea that back-to-back short and simple sentences sound simplistic, but a single simple sentence following a string of complex sentences pops. For instance, in this concluding paragraph, a short, punchy sentence lends finality where a longer sentence would not:

> **All in all, the Anti-Federalists make the stronger argument. The Federalist argument makes sense only when national security means not only defending the country against external threats, but quelling internal conflicts and pursuing national glory as well. Ultimately, I think that the argument for imbuing the national government with unlimited powers is really an argument for national glory, and in that respect I agree wholeheartedly with Brutus when he says, "Let the monarchs keep it!" The most reasonable argument, though, comes from Patrick Henry, who suggests, "Too much suspicion may be corrected. If you give too little power to-day, you may give more to-morrow. But the reverse of the proposition will not hold. If you give too much power to-day, you cannot retake it to-morrow. This," Henry says, "no man can deny."**

Emphasis and Parallel Structures

The second way to attain resonance in a concluding sentence is to express ideas with a precisely parallel structure as close to the ending as possible so that the important ideas are the last ones readers see. For instance, compare these two sentences:

- **Emphasis, pithy wording, and resonance make for good conclusions.**
- **Good conclusions demonstrate emphasis, pithiness, and resonance.**

Which ideas resonate most in each? Which feels more conclusive? For me, the second sentence is more emphatic and conclusive. The three parallel ideas feel like an ending. Now consider the effect of these sentences:

- **Good conclusions demonstrate emphasis, pithiness, and resonance, too.**
- **Good conclusions demonstrate not only emphasis and pithiness, but resonance as well.**

In the first sentence, the final 'too' leaches emphasis away, but in the second sentence, the 'not only_____, but _____ as well' construction adds emphasis to the final idea of 'resonance.'

Finally, while all parallel structures emphasize ideas, the more precisely parallel these structures are, the more the ideas resonate. For example, if a writer composes a sentence with three direct objects but applies an adjective to just one of them, the sentence falls flat:

- **Quality writing demonstrates clarity, coherent progressions, and eloquence.**

The sentence is improved by adding an adjective for the other objects:

- **Quality writing demonstrates clear content, coherent progressions, and eloquent prose.**

An even more rhetorically effective strategy involves adding an additional qualifier to the last item:

- **Quality writing demonstrates clear content, coherent progressions, and eloquent, resonant prose.**

Needless to say, not every idea in an essay merits emphasis. In an academic essay, most of the emphasis falls at the end of paragraphs, although not every paragraph will necessarily seem or feel conclusive. Consider, for instance, the difference between an introductory paragraph that concludes with a thesis statement and one that ends with a statement of intent. The thesis statement clearly identifies the writer's main idea, potentially naming three points, and hopefully using parallel structure. Such a statement will feel important; the paragraph will seem conclusive—unsupported, yes, but conclusive. The statement of intent, on the other hand, merely says, "This paper will discuss X." The reader must continue reading to come to any conclusion.

In the same way, body paragraphs may or may not require any wrap-up. Often, this will depend on the intended effect of each paragraph in the essay's logical progression. For instance, in an essay that relates events following a chronological order, the writer may omit a wrap-up at the end of each paragraph, which will recount events that perhaps had no real conclusion—and that makes sense, because in real life, history happens fluidly, with no neat paragraph breaks. On the other hand, in an essay following a causal order, the writer's points might build upon one another in such a way that the reader must agree with the point made in the first paragraph in order to understand the point that will be made in the second. In such an essay, reiterating the point being made in each paragraph is vital.

In order to assess the quality of concluding statements in your student's papers, try circling the final three to five words of a paragraph and consider whether these represent the ideas that are most significant to the paragraph's purpose. Consider also whether the paragraph's most significant ideas involve one element, in which case the final element will probably be best expressed in a single, resonant statement; or more than one element, in which case the sentence structure should be perfectly parallel, with elements each getting equal billing—that is, if one element consists of a phrase, all elements consist of phrases, and if one element is a clause, all elements consist of clauses.

Generating the Rubric

The rubrics you generated to address issues affecting clarity and coherence focused primarily on correcting problematic patterns. Generating this rubric will be a little different in that the only potential problem here is faulty rhythm. The better part of the rubric will actually involve designing goals to encourage students to apply new skills such as combining sentences gracefully and concluding paragraphs emphatically. For instance, you might design a goal that encourages students to use parallel structures more purposefully:

Category & Criteria	Unacceptable; needs revision	Acceptable; meets the standard	Excellent; exceeds the standard
Eloquence: Sentence Structure	The students' use of parallel structures seems haphazard and is reflected only in simple sentences with compound elements	The student uses parallel structures in at least three distinct grammatical structures in the essay	The student uses parallel structures in at least five distinct ways in the essay, including at least two parallel phrases or clauses

Another appropriate goal might encourage the use of colons or semi-colons:

Category & Criteria	Unacceptable; needs revision	Acceptable; meets the standard	Excellent; exceeds the standard
Conventions: Capitalization	The student includes no colons or semi-colons in the essay OR the student uses colons and semi-colons incorrectly	The student correctly uses at least one colon or semi-colon in the essay	The student correctly uses both colons and semi-colons in the essay

By now, you should be seeing apparent growth in your student's essay writing skills. Your student's conclusions should be getting stronger—although of all of the items in this chapter, resonant conclusions will develop slowest, since rhetorical power is more challenging to attain than grammatical symmetry. On this item, I would encourage you to be patient—and if you feel that students are overdoing their efforts at eloquence, be ready to explain why. Praise the attempt, but discuss how overblown rhetoric affects you as a reader. In my experience, most students appreciate honest appraisal—and they usually agree when something's exaggerated in their writing, but they resent unsupported criticism.

Basically, as your student practices to perfect his or her writing skills, your job is to be a coach, cheering when something is done exceptionally well, and working with your student to figure out how to perfect steps, strokes, or swings that are somehow off. Describe yourself as a reader, not a judge, and describe your reactions with authority—because you are, in fact, a reader. Students appreciate the difference between thoughtful feedback and unreasonable demands, and they're much more likely to apply reasonable advice than what feels like unreasonable criticism.

At this point, students know how to write academic essays to inform, explain, persuade, and analyze topics; they have learned the necessary principles to write clearly, coherently, and eloquently. In short, they have learned everything they need in order to write competently for any functional purpose life can throw their way. Now all they need to do to cement this learning is practice.

Eloquent Prose Rubric

Criteria	Unacceptable	Acceptable	Excellent
Clarity: Subjects and Verbs	The writer conveys meaning through nominalizations, adjectives and adverbs; verbs are nondescript (i.e., have, make, do, be) or weak in five or more sentences per page	The writer prefers the use of clear subjects and active verbs but includes up to three sentences per page with unnecessary expletive construction, passive voice, or weak or nondescript verbs	The writer prefers to write with clear subjects and active verbs and can justify any use of the passive voice or expletive construction; no verbs are weak or nondescript
Clarity: Sentence correctness	Some sentences run on or are incomplete; sentences contain more than 5 errors in spelling, capitalization, or punctuation per page	Sentences are complete and demonstrate no more than 3 errors in spelling, capitalization, or punctuation per page	Sentences are complete and demonstrate no more than 1 error of any kind per page
Coherence: Thoroughness and Order of Support	Sentences do not reflect any logical order, appear to be out-of-order or off-topic, and/or include logical gaps or redundancies	Sentences reflect a logical order and initiate with previously introduced ideas and establish new ideas; any gap or overlap of ideas is slight	Sentences occur in a logical order and establish new ideas; the writer interrupts this progression only to clarify or qualify points when necessary
Eloquence: Sentence length and type	Sentences are of similar length and type; sequential sentences repeat the same patterns and seem choppy or monotonous	Sentence length is mostly long; sentences do not repeat the same patterns but each paragraph includes some variety	Sentence length is generally long but some paragraphs include a short emphatic sentence; at least three distinct sentence structures are present in each paragraph
Eloquence: Parallel Structures	Sentences include grammatically awkward structures that could be resolved with a parallel structure	Sentences use grammatically appropriate parallel structures	Sentences generally use grammatically correct parallel structures; a few precisely balanced parallel ideas add rhythm and emphasis
Eloquence: Resonant Endings	Concluding words are lackluster, lacking significance, parallel structure, or intrigue	Concluding sentences shift important words to the final position	Concluding sentences shift important words to the final position; parallel structures are well-balanced; a few pithy statements are intriguing or powerful

Eloquent Prose Checklist

Parallel Grammatical Elements

☐ Does the student combine sentences with the same subjects and verbs?

☐ Does the student use colons and semi-colons to show the relationship of ideas in independent clauses (i.e., complete sentences)?

☐ Does the student include compound subjects, verbs, and direct objects as well as parallel phrases and clauses to convey logically equivalent ideas?

Natural Rhythm

☐ Do paragraphs flow smoothly and avoid awkward, choppy, or monotonous rhythms?

☐ Do paragraphs include sentences of varied length and complexity?

☐ Does the student vary the way sentences begin?

Appropriate Emphasis

☐ Do sentences begin with old information and lead to new?

☐ Do paragraphs that make a point lead readers to it?

☐ Do paragraphs that make a point include a wrap-up statement?

☐ Do concluding wrap-up statements end with the important ideas?

☐ Does the final, concluding statement for the essay achieve resonance with either a short, punchy statement or a precisely parallel structure?

Part 2

Advanced Compositions

for

College-Bound Students

Chapter 9

Beyond Five Paragraphs

Until now, students have focused on learning the essential skills that anyone needs to communicate ideas in writing. This section of the book deals with compositions and skills that serve specifically academic purposes. That is to say, only people who are writing for an academic purpose or audience take on the writing tasks described in the next three chapters. Presumably, only students who intend to attend college in the near future will see the point of tackling them.

Ideally, every high school student will attempt at least one lengthy composition before graduating; however, I would advise you to retain the five-paragraph essay form until your student can consistently write with clarity, coherence, and eloquence. For students who have not mastered these by their senior year of high school, a research paper will present a formidable challenge; still, such a student might attempt such a project with support. For instance, you might break tasks down into manageable pieces and assign due dates for each. That way, students make progress toward the goal without feeling overwhelmed.

THE IMPORTANCE OF STUDENT CHOICE

One of the most significant distinctions between this section and the previous one is that here students should select topics for compositions freely. Whereas basic compositions required students to attain the ability to respond to any academic prompt, just as in college they will be forced to respond to their professors' assignments and in life they will be forced to respond to whatever situations arise, these assignments demand a great deal of personal investment. Students must be given freedom to choose not only their topics, but also their sources; they must be allowed to interpret material for themselves and come to their own conclusions. Anything less is but another version of summary.

That is not to say that you will no longer assign prompts for five-paragraph essays; rather, academic prompts for five-paragraph essays will now be limited to those topics for which you need to document your student's learning. For instance, you might assign an academic prompt to a student studying economics to challenge him or her to apply the concept of price ceilings to the housing market in your community. The essay provides documentation for your records and challenges your student to think about how economics apply to real-world situations.

What you will no longer do is assign academic prompts for five-paragraph essays for the essays' sake alone. By the time your student reaches this advanced level, he or she will have achieved basic competency in composing essays, and you no longer need to provide opportunities for him or her to practice that skill. Instead, the opportunities you provide will center on the advanced compositions described in these chapters, which, unlike five-paragraph essays, each require extended periods of time to compose. Thus students should not be expected to produce great quantities of advanced compositions, but rather students should be allowed sufficient time to research or read, to compose, to revise, and to edit compositions for the qualities they have learned.

Reasonable expectations at this level depend on the student. A student who reads and writes quickly might compose as many as four literary analyses and two research or argument papers per year; students who read and write more slowly might accomplish half as much. Again, I would only reiterate that quantity matters far less at this level than quality: think of these compositions as capstone projects, the fruit of eleven or twelve long years of education. Allow your student to delve deeply and to enjoy learning and producing projects of which he or she can be proud. Provide support, but avoid putting on unnecessary pressure. If these projects are the fruit of your student's efforts, they are also the fruit of yours. Enjoy them.

USING RUBRICS AT THE ADVANCED LEVEL

Unlike before, for this and all advanced level compositions you won't need to generate writing samples, although you may continue to individualize rubrics if certain issues still fluster your student. Otherwise, you can opt to use the Literary Analysis, Research Paper, and Researched Argument rubrics found in the corresponding chapters. The objectives for these rubrics combine the broad criteria from the basic composition course with skills that pertain to each type of advanced composition. The Literary Analysis Rubric on page 118, for instance, includes one criterion each for clarity, coherence, and eloquence as well as three criteria that apply specifically to literary analyses: identification of a literary work's author and title, correct citations, and appropriate support from the literary work itself for the writer's assertions about the text.

Expansive Writing Purposes

The literary analysis, research paper, and researched argument tasks challenge students to abandon the now familiar five-paragraph essay form and write more expansively about topics that require extensive research. What makes these compositions so challenging is the increased need for engaging rhetoric and eloquent style, combined with the need to organize copious amounts of information. On top of all that, students must now incorporate material from outside, authoritative sources. Citing these sources correctly complicates what by now has become a fairly comfortable task.

All three advanced writing applications require significant student commitment. Whereas a five-paragraph essay rarely calls for more than cursory research, both arguments and research papers demand that students gather multiple resources and consider them carefully. A literary analysis, while potentially less demanding, may also require reading and re-reading a significant literary work. Such projects take time, as in an entire quarter or semester, as opposed to the week or two that a five-paragraph essay usually takes.

Moving Beyond the Five-Paragraph Form

By the time students arrive at the advanced level, they will be very familiar with the five-paragraph form, and happily, that familiarity will be useful to them, as many of the essential features of a five-paragraph essay will be retained in lengthier compositions. Thesis statements, topic sentences (for some if not all paragraphs), and the concept of having three solid points of support for any point or assertion continue to apply; the formulation of the thesis, the necessity of background information, and the adjustment from thinking in terms of paragraphs to thinking in sections now change.

A Word about Formatting

Until now, I have not mentioned formatting, which is a trivial matter when assignments are written solely to turn in to a teacher and no one else. But as students move on to longer compositions, their efforts will merit preservation and, potentially, dissemination. College administrators, for instance, may request a sample of the student's writing, and a composition that demonstrates a higher level of complexity will be more impressive than a simple five-paragraph exposition. Therefore, for compositions at the advanced level, students should format essays appropriately: compositions should be typed and printed on standard white 8 ½ x 11 paper in an easy-to-read font (11 or 12 point Times New Roman and Arial are two examples); margins should be set at 1" on all sides, and lines should be double spaced. That much is more or less standard. MLA (Modern Language Association), which is the documentation style I would recommend for college-bound high school students, requires students to add a header in the upper right hand corner (½" from the top of the page) that includes their last name, two spaces, and then the page number. On the first four lines of the first page, students should list their name, their teacher's name, the course name, and the date. The next line should give the paper's title, centered, and the actual composition will begin, left-justified, on the line after that.

ARGUMENT FORM

Just as a five-paragraph essay provides a convenient and flexible form for any simple academic writing task, the classical argument form does the same thing for compositions that require more development. The argument form provides a reliable framework for organizing large amounts of information coherently and helps students avoid wasting time trying to figure out how to order ideas without leaving holes, straying off topic, or including redundancies. Although most appropriate to arguments, the argument form can be helpful in whole or in part for students attempting to organize information for other purposes, such as writing a literary analysis or a research paper, as well as for functional purposes such as applying to college or writing letters of complaint. By providing a framework for organizing information into five sections, the argument form eliminates a lot of hassle that might otherwise trip students up.

Conveniently, the argument form is similar to the five-paragraph essay in that students can continue to think in terms of fives; however, the argument form is distinct in that rather than paragraphs, the student must now think in terms of sections that accomplish specific purposes. The five sections in an argument tend to be more extensive than paragraphs in a five-paragraph essay, even when the function of the paragraph and section is the same.

For instance, the introduction in an argument has a more sophisticated purpose than the introduction in a simple five-paragraph essay. Whereas an essay writer needs only to provide some "hook" for a reader, with the argument form, a writer needs to appeal to the reader's sense of morality or elicit a sympathetic response, often by narrating a true story that touches on the topic in some way. Thus the introduction assigns a moral significance to the essay topic before adding some kind of commentary to either provide context or to bridge the gap between the introductory story and the thesis statement. Of course, there remains the option of using an announcement of intent in place of the thesis statement at the end of the introduction; however, unless the student is writing inductively—that is, writing in order to discover his or her own conclusion—a thesis statement is preferable.

The next three sections of the argument each serve distinct purposes: the second section, which is usually just a paragraph or two, provides background information about the essay topic; the third section develops the main argument about the topic; the fourth section acknowledges and refutes any opposition to the writer's position. Let's take a closer look at each of these paragraphs.

Following the introduction is a section that provides the reader with any information necessary to understand the argument the writer is about to make. This is different from the five-paragraph essay, in which the thesis (which is usually the last element of the introduction) is followed immediately by the first point in support of the thesis statement. In an argument, the introduction concludes with a thesis that specifies what the writer is about to argue, but instead of immediately starting to argue, the writer puts that argument on hold in order to provide any definitions, facts, statistics, or historical context that the reader will need to understand in order to follow the writer's argument.

The background information section reduces the need to continually interrupt the progression of an argument to define terms or explain parenthetical details, but some students feel confused about what goes in it. Students might want to consider writing their argument first; then, once it's clear what material is parenthetical to the main argument, move those details to the background information section later. For instance, say a student finds that he or she must continually interrupt the progression of a paragraph in the argument section to provide historical details that explain why something happened or how something came to be. In that situation, dedicating a paragraph or two in the background section to chronicling the history of the topic would allow the argument section to flow more smoothly. Similarly, students might find themselves pausing to continually define unusual terms or provide important statistics. Depending on the topic, the background information section can be a convenient dumping place for any of these, allowing the rest of the composition to progress more coherently.

The third section contains the argument itself. Assuming the thesis contains three reasons for the position taken, this section would contain three paragraphs supporting each of those points and more if arbitrary paragraphing becomes necessary (see the next section for more about arbitrary paragraphing). In a sense, this section is more or less equivalent to the entire body of a five-paragraph essay, since its purpose is to provide reasonable support for the thesis statement.

Sections of an Argument

Introduction

Purpose: Introduce the topic with an appeal to emotion

Transitions to the body of the composition and ends with a thesis statement

Length: 1 – 3 paragraphs, depending on the length of the composition

---

Background Information

Purpose: Provides facts, statistics, definitions or history that enables readers to understand the argument or discussion that follows

Length: 1 – 3 paragraphs, depending on the complexity of the topic

---

Argument

Purpose: **in an argument,** this section provides persuasive reasons for accepting the writer's argument; **in a research paper,** this section presents information reflecting one of two perspectives about a controversial subject

Length: approximately 3 true paragraphs, more if arbitrary paragraphing is employed

---

Counterargument

Purpose: **in an argument,** this section acknowledges opposing viewpoints and explains why these do not negate the argument; **in a research paper,** this section presents information about the other main viewpoint about the issue being discussed

Length: 1 – 2 paragraphs in an argument; the same as the argument in a research paper

---

Conclusion

Purpose: reiterates main points of the argument (or in a research paper, reiterates both perspectives), and *draws a conclusion*; in most cases, the final paragraph reiterates the rhetorical appeal from the introduction and ends on a resonant note

Length: usually 1 – 2 paragraphs, depending on the length of the composition

Following the argument is the counterargument. This section involves either acknowledging weaknesses in the writer's argument and explaining why these weaknesses do not negate the validity of the argument or responding to people whose objections are predictable and explaining why the position taken by the student is superior. Usually, this section will contain either the same number of paragraphs as the argument or slightly fewer, since a strong argument by definition contains more points in its favor than the opposition.

In a research paper, this section will simply provide the opposite perspective in equal measure to the information provided for the first perspective in the argument section. In other words, when working with a research paper, the two sections might be thought of as "Argument 1" and "Argument 2." The two perspectives should contain approximately the same amount of information and be about the same length.

The conclusion section allows the writer to reiterate main points and draw a conclusion. In a research paper, the student will truly draw a conclusion: having discussed two sides of a controversial issue, the conclusion will be where the writer highlights the most important evidence and announce what he or she has come up with as a result. On the other hand, in an argument, the student will have known the conclusion from the beginning and will be attempting more to reiterate main points in one final attempt to convince the reader as well.

An effective conclusion will often recall the images and ideas set forth in the introduction; it might even complete a story initiated earlier. Whatever else it does, the conclusion should reiterate the significance of the argument in some way that connects with readers morally and emotionally. The final sentence of this conclusion, much more so than the conclusions in five-paragraph essays, should definitely resonate.

ARBITRARY PARAGRAPHING

As students mature in their writing and thinking skills, their ideas and assertions grow more complex, requiring more definition and support than simpler ones and resulting in longer paragraphs than before. For the most part, a paragraph that develops a complex idea extensively but not redundantly is a good thing. It means the student is writing with greater sophistication, and that is exactly what you would expect to see.

The problem with paragraphs that get very long—as in more than half a page of text—is that they tend to daunt readers. Something about a large block of text with no visual break bothers readers. Some people, seeing a gigantic paragraph, automatically skip ahead to the next section or start to skim. Knowing this, most experienced writers try to prevent scaring off readers by arbitrarily breaking super-long paragraphs into more manageable units.

Arbitrary paragraphing can be somewhat confusing for students because it means that no longer will their paragraphs all include topic sentences. Up to this point, students will have begun each body paragraph with a topic sentence which they will have followed with a clear and orderly progression of ideas. As writing becomes more sophisticated, however, ideas become more complex and require more extensive clarification and support, sometimes increasing the length of paragraphs beyond the half-page mark. This is when students need to start using their own judgment to decide when and where a paragraph needs to be divided.

Arbitrary paragraphing permits writers to be thorough in their support of ideas without the text on the page appearing to visually drone, but it's important to break paragraphs at a logical place: arbitrary doesn't mean random. For instance, in the case of a long paragraph containing multiple narrative examples, each narrative could be its own paragraph. In that case, the three examples support a single purpose, which in theory should all occur within a single paragraph, but the necessity of retaining a comfortable reading format for the reader compels the writer to break the paragraph arbitrarily.

If you peruse almost any newspaper, magazine, or online article, you'll see that most paragraphing in the real world is arbitrary. The reason students don't need such long paragraphs before this point is that younger students rarely have the capacity to develop such complex thoughts or understand how to support assertions as thoroughly as coherence demands. When your student reaches the point where arbitrarily breaking paragraphs becomes necessary, he or she has achieved milestone as a thinker and as a writer.

Chapter 10

Literary Analysis

Because literary analysis affords the most natural bridge between basic and advanced writing purposes, I recommend introducing it before either the researched argument or research paper. A literary analysis can be a fairly simple five-paragraph essay (such as the essay, "Attitudes about Education" found in Appendix D) or a relatively complex analysis of perhaps five to seven pages. (Of course, a literary analysis can be longer, but no reason compels a high school student to write more than five pages or so unless he or she wants to.)

A literary analysis is not a book report, which is a formulaic summary of a book's basic elements and a relatively cursory evaluation. Rather, a literary analysis is a writer's attempt to evaluate or critically explore some aspect of a literary work in depth. Mortimer Adler and Charles Van Doren (1972) suggest that mature understanding results in a reader's evaluation becoming more analytical:

> You will say not only that you like or dislike the book, but also why. The reasons
> you give will, of course, have some critical relevance to the book itself, but in
> their first expression they are more likely to be about you—your preferences and
> prejudices—than about the book. Hence, to complete the task of criticism, you
> must objectify your reactions by pointing to those things in the book that
> caused them. You must pass from saying what you like or dislike and why, to
> saying what is good or bad about the book and why. (p. 214)

Thus a literary analysis is an evaluation of a book based on reasons rather than taste alone. For instance, on a shallow level, a reader might say that he liked *Murder on the Orient Express* because it was a pretty good mystery as far as mysteries go. And a reader is entitled to an opinion of this sort; however, it is just an opinion; it reflects only the reader's taste. A more thoughtful response might include more specific details about why *Murder on the Orient Express* is a good mystery, complete with examples about precisely what made it effective. That each of Poirot's suspects seemed guilty at different times, that specific details that led the reader to think so—this is a more analytical response.

Because literary analysis involves supporting a theory about a literary work with evidence from the text, part of the challenge in writing one is incorporating material from the work in question gracefully and responsibly. In a simple literary analysis, students may stick to summarizing pertinent episodes and paraphrasing speech, which does not necessarily require quoting the literary work in the text of the paper. Eventually, though, students who develop more substantial assertions will need to support them with evidence from the text, including relevant quotations. What makes incorporating these quotations challenging is discerning exactly how much of a passage to include. Quoting entire sentences when a phrase would suffice confounds the writer's purpose in choosing it and reflects a lack of discrimination that readers of an analysis paper typically expect.

I don't recommend students attempting to write a literary analysis of any complexity until the junior year of high school at earliest. The first two to three years of high school are best spent building up a propensity to read good literature with breadth and depth so that by the final years of high school, students are ready and eager to explore more challenging literature that has the capacity to intrigue and enrich them. Most freshmen and sophomores aren't ready to explore sophisticated themes or appreciate the challenging literature that contains them. Of course, you may assign literary analyses considerably sooner if you as their teacher (or some curriculum you buy) dictate what students are to write in their analysis, but what would be the point? Writing down someone else's analysis of a literary work is not doing analysis, it's summarizing information. Regurgitating other people's literary interpretations does little to develop a student's own critical thinking skills, and such exercises prohibit students from exploring the ideas in literature that intrigue them personally, which is the only real reason for anyone to engage in literary analysis. It is far better for younger students to develop skills in discussing literature by writing brief summaries and reviews and hold off analyses until they've gained the sophistication that comes with maturity and experience to analyze literature for themselves.

QUESTIONS TO EXPLORE IN A LITERARY ANALYSIS:

A genuine literary analysis allows students to explore what they find fascinating. For instance, a literary analysis might explore the meaning or effectiveness of a literary work; examine how an author achieved a certain effect; analyze how certain actions result in good or evil or how the author uses certain people, places, or things to symbolize deeper themes; compare two or more literary works; or draw evidence from outside sources in order to evaluate the validity or effectiveness of some aspect of the literary work in question.

What was the author trying to say with this literary work?

The student might attempt to answer this question by exploring a theme the author seems to be grappling with or by exploring the author's juxtaposition of the protagonist's values versus those of the antagonist. Another option here is to do a little research about the author's situation—was the author responding to a contemporary situation or a new philosophy? Such research can be as simple as looking up the author on Wikipedia and, if the information there is sufficiently intriguing, pursuing further investigation elsewhere.

What techniques did the author use to accomplish a certain effect?

The student might explore an author's use of figurative language, allusion, flashbacks or foreshadowing, or point-of-view for telling a story.

How does the work compare with a similar work?

The student might explore similarities or differences between two books that struck him or her as particularly alike in some way.

How does the work reflect or challenge the values of society?

Many books are classic because they changed the way people thought. The student might consider how a work like Sinclair's *The Jungle* challenged society at the time it was written; alternatively, a student might explore how a classic work would challenge the values evident in our society, today.

How well did the author accomplish his or her purposes?

The student might consider whether the work meets the two criteria for successful fiction: whether or not it is believable, and whether or not it affects a reader emotionally. Believability means that the characters, situation, and setting of the story do not get in the way of the reader's ability to get into the story. Notice here that believable does not mean plausible: even the imaginary characters and settings in works such as Tolkien's *The Lord of the Rings* feel believable because of their realistic depiction. Also, believability means that the reader feels as though the events in the story are plausible within the story world; they don't feel contrived by the author. For instance, I have noticed that some works of historical fiction feel implausible; they feel as though someone stuffed a bunch of characters and events into a particular historical timeframe primarily to educate me about that time, rather than because the author had a real story to tell. I've also read books where I read a scene and felt like the author was deliberately attempting to advance his or her agenda through it. Such scenes preach rather than depict, and they strike me as contrived. I find that I usually don't like those books very well, even if I agree with the author's agenda. They simply don't strike me as believable fiction.

The other quality by which works of fiction are evaluated is whether they have the power to affect the reader: to make the reader feel something for or about the characters involved. Obviously, if a book bores readers, it is not very successful. My five-star book rating almost always means a book has made me either laugh out loud or cry, and often both. For instance, when I read *All Quiet on the Western Front*, it made me laugh and cry at different points in the narrative. I rate the book highly because it affected me deeply.

Deductive and Inductive Analysis

In a literary analysis, a student explores some intriguing aspect of a literary work either deductively or inductively. According to English education professors Harold Vine and Mark Faust (1993), "being deductive means that the meaning maker [i.e., the student] begins with a hypothesis and attends to only those details that support it" (p. 107). In contrast, "inductive thinkers regard their initial sense of the situation as tentative and open to revision as new and unanticipated aspects arise" (p. 108).

In other words, students can choose to either develop a thesis statement about a literary work and then support that thesis in the body of their essay, or students can introduce some aspect of a literary work that they wish to further explore in writing and let the paper develop with their thoughts. An example of a deductive literary analysis can be found in the essay, "Good and Evil in *The Lord of the Rings*," found in Appendix D; an example of an inductive literary analysis appears at the end of this chapter.

INCORPORATING QUOTATIONS

A literary analysis is the best way to introduce the challenge of incorporating quotations to a piece of writing because it accustoms students to quoting materials in a very limited way. In a literary analysis, students learn how to integrate both short and long quotations appropriately and to distinguish clearly between summaries, paraphrases, and quotations, but since most literary analyses will involve only one or maybe two or three sources, students may focus on basic documentation rather than on the fastidious rules that apply to citing the many different types of sources students will encounter with research papers and arguments. Thus the initial challenge for students involves identifying sources simply and incorporating content from authoritative sources judiciously.

Identify the Literary Work and its Author

In a literary analysis, the topic of the paper is the literary work itself. This facilitates the first criteria for responsible documentation, which is clarifying the source. Simply name the author(s) and title of the work(s) in the introduction, as in this introductory paragraph, which includes the title and author of a literary work, a brief summary, and a thesis statement:

> In his book, *The Curious Incident of the Dog in the Night-time*, Mark Haddon depicts a fifteen-year-old autistic boy as a superbly logical detective sleuth who sets out to discover who killed the neighbor's dog with a garden fork, a mystery which ultimately leads him to discover the continued existence of the mother he previously thought dead. Although Haddon's portrayal of the character Christopher meets many criteria for autism, Haddon slightly misrepresents autism in a number of ways that are not immediately apparent upon a superficial reading but become more so upon analysis.

Support Assertions with Evidence from the Literary Work

The most authoritative support in a literary analysis always comes from the literary work itself; nevertheless, the majority of sentences in a literary analysis should take the form of summary generated by the student, not quotations taken directly from the text. In fact, students should limit direct quotations from the text to the few lines that support points directly and convincingly. The better part of a literary analysis should be the writer's support for assertions in the form of summarized events and paraphrased utterances from the text.

> Autism is typified by restricted interests, while Christopher's interests are quite diverse. This is not immediately apparent from the book: one's first impression is that Christopher's interests are limited to mathematics, video games, and his pet rat, Toby. However, a closer reading reveals that this is hardly the case. Between action scenes, Haddon intersperses a number of flashbacks and parenthetical commentaries that reveal Christopher's knowledge of such disparate disciplines as astronomy, cardiology, Greek, geography, logic, literature, probability, Latin, theoretical physics, etymology, and entomology. Considering the reduced curriculum taught in Christopher's school, combined with the improbable depth of his father's library, one has to wonder where Christopher has been learning dead languages like Greek and Latin, not to mention theoretical physics. Christopher would have to be hyperlexic as well as savant in the areas of mathematical calculation, mapping, and drawing. Although I will not argue that Haddon's character is impossibly unrealistic, such an array of talents would certainly be improbable.

Furthermore, students should be judicious with quotations. A common mistake among students writing literary analyses for the first time is to support assertions with extensive quotations from the text; unfortunately, long quotations sometimes detract from the coherence of a literary analysis because students often judge the completeness of their essays by length, and since long quotations take up a lot of space on paper, they assume the long quotation adequately supports a point that summarizing two or three incidents would support better.

Another problem with quoting entire incidents or speeches involves the extraneous material in the quote. Rarely does a long passage support only the assertion a writer wants to make about it. As a result, long quotations often become unwieldy and confuse readers, who may or may not see precisely which part of the long quote the writer intended as support for his or her own point. So not only are quotations rarely necessary, long quotations are even less so. Most assertions in literary analyses are best supported with short excerpts, usually less than a sentence in length, as in this quotation:

> **Interestingly, Haddon's first person character never indicates any emotion nor initiates any affectionate behavior toward his father or anyone else. Instead, Christopher responds to his father's spread-out hand-touching ritual "because sometimes Father wants to give me a hug, but I do not like hugging people so we do this instead, and it means that he loves me" (16).**

Finally, students should use an ellipsis to exclude impertinent parts of the quoted material, and, should the quotation contain confusing wording such as a pronoun whose antecedent is not included in the quote, students can use brackets to adjust the quotation for purposes of clarification:

> **Temple Grandin indicates that it is not the lack of primary social emotions that identify individuals with autism, but the inability to experience ambiguity among such emotions. For instance, individuals with autism don't experience mixed emotions such as love-hate: "A child can be furious at his mom or dad one second, then completely forget about it the next," but "when [an adult who doesn't have autism] gets furiously angry with a person he loves, his brain hooks up anger and love and remembers it . . . his brain learns to have mixed emotions" (90). According to Grandin, people with autism never experience this kind of ambiguity.**

Literary Analysis Rubric

For this essay, you have two choices: either combine criteria from previous levels, highlighting one or two specific goals your student continues to struggle with, or use the Literary Analysis Rubric found on page 118.

Literary Analysis Checklist

Analysis

☐ Does the student explore a specific question or aspect of the literary work?

☐ Does the student state a position and then support it in a deductive analysis?

☐ Does the student announce an intention to explore an idea inductively?

☐ Does the student cite evidence from the text to support assertions?

Content

☐ Are the literary work and author identified in the introduction?

☐ Does the student rely primarily on summary and paraphrase when citing evidence?

☐ Does the student incorporate quotations judiciously?

☐ Does the student avoid quoting more text than that which provides specific support for his or her points?

Documentation

☐ Does the student indicate page numbers where quotations were found?

☐ Does the student include a bibliography?

☐ Does the student correctly format the paper as a whole? In-text citations? The bibliography?

SAMPLE LITERARY ANALYSIS

To give you an idea of what a literary analysis might look like, I include an example of an inductive literary analysis in which I explore an issue that intrigued me about a literary work. This essay includes a number of characteristics you would expect to see in a literary analysis: appropriate formatting (though with a few deviations, such as the absence of an MLA-appropriate header and space-and-a-half rather than double-spacing), subtle thesis and topic sentences, evidence summarized and quoted from the text in question and outside resources, citations in the text, and a bibliography at the end.

Dena Luchsinger

Ms. Bauer

Advanced Composition

21 June 2012

Why Cassie Died:

An Exploration of a Modern Tragedy

Harriet Arnow's *The Dollmaker* can only be described as a tragedy. The novel begins during World War II, with Gertie Nevels and her family barely getting by as sharecroppers in rural Kentucky. Though life is hard, Gertie loves the land and doesn't mind having to work hard to raise crops. Her husband Clovis hauls coal in the pickup truck he keeps running with his mechanical skills. Unlike Gertie, Clovis resents his lot in life. When Clovis gets called up for military duty, he takes off for factory work in Detroit, where he believes he can earn more money. He sends for his family after he gets settled, but moving to Detroit means that Gertie, who inherited money from her brother, has to relinquish the property she purchased with her inheritance in Clovis' absence. Though she hates to give up the land, Gertie moves her family to Detroit, where she feels cooped up in her little house. Nothing she does turns out well in spite of the modern conveniences Clovis buys for her on credit, and her children struggle to adjust to life in the city. Eventually her oldest son runs away, and later, her daughter Cassie dies in a train accident. Then Clovis loses his job, and the entire family has to find ways to earn money. The move to Detroit leaves the family divided, destitute, and broken; and as a reader, I wanted somebody to blame.

For the better part of the book, I hated Clovis for his selfishness and stupidity. What kind of man moves to Detroit without even consulting his wife first or asking how she feels about it? I wondered how anyone could be so stupid as to think that modern conveniences and more money would make up for a dreary life in the city. That Clovis seemed to think that Gertie would be pleased with his arrangements and that his kids would adjust to city life only proved to me that he never took the time to understand his own wife and kids. If someone is to blame for everything that Gertie suffers in Detroit, Clovis seems like the perfect choice.

Only later in the book did I realize that Clovis is as much a victim of circumstance as Gertie. When Clovis leaves Kentucky, he wants only to provide a better life for his wife and kids. To him, that meant that his wife would not have to labor in fields and do chores that modern women didn't have to do. "Meg's seen an easier life than you," he says sadly the day he leaves home; "No heaven and sweaten fer her to make corn grow in land that ud be better left in scrub pine and saw briers" (84). Clovis knows that he can't improve Gertie's life in Kentucky, so he takes the initiative of moving to a place where he can. He doesn't ask his wife if he should try to provide for his family; back then, a man was supposed to provide for his family if by any means he could. Clovis thinks Gertie will be happier with fewer chores, so he feels confused and hurt when nothing he buys to reduce Gertie's workload seems to please her. Clovis does the best he can to be a good husband, which is probably why Clovis turns to violence when his job is threatened by talk of a union strike: once again, circumstances beyond his control threaten his ability to provide for his family. What choice does he have? By the end of the novel, Clovis has become an even more tragic figure than Gertie.

Another obvious source of blame is Gertie's mother. It's hard to imagine a more disagreeable person. She lives in relative comfort, and she does little to help Gertie with her large family. When Gertie's son nearly dies of diphtheria, Gertie's mother complains that Gertie didn't visit her during her own, milder illness. Worst of all, Gertie's mother bullies Gertie into relinquishing the land she bought with her inheritance, saying Clovis "ain't no farmer . . . [You've] held him back all these years" (142). Gertie wants to stay, but almost immediately, the man who sold her the land appears, saying, "Yer Mom sent fer me yisterday. From the way she talks a body ud think I was maken a mint a money out a sellen that land" (145). Keeping the land no longer an option, Gertie has no choice but to follow Clovis to Detroit.

Or does she? Gertie's twelve-year-old son Rueben wears his disappointment openly when she doesn't defend her dreams: "with no more words and never a look for Gertie [Reuben] led the gray mule barnward" (144). Clearly, Reuben believes his mother had a choice in the matter, and Gertie later learns that Reuben was right. After Cassie dies, crushed by a train, Clovis says, "Why, if I'd ha knowed you'd ha had all that money, I'd said buy a place an wait fer me. I'd ha worked up here jist long enough to git me a pretty good truck an soon as th war was over I'd come a rollen home" (426). Of course, Clovis may or may not have been expressing what really would have happened, but Gertie herself realizes that her secrecy led to their ruin, and she hates herself "who had caused it all" (417).

And yet, if it is hard to blame Clovis, it's even harder to blame Gertie. By the end of the novel, she's lost her dream, her hope, and the two children dearest to her. No, Gertie's willingness to hate and blame herself for everything makes me want to exonerate her for her keeping the money she'd saved a secret. And while it's impossible to like Gertie's mother, Gertie herself acknowledges that she was right to advise Gertie to move when she meets her scantily clad, next-door neighbor.

In the end, it's hard to find anyone to blame for the tragedy. According to Mortimer Adler and Charles Van Doren, "the essence of tragedy is time, or rather the lack of it" (227). Had Gertie bought the land before Clovis had to leave, the family might never have had to move. Had Gertie understood how precious Cassie's imaginary friend Callie Lou was sooner, Cassie might never have hid near the train. Had Gertie reached Cassie sooner, she might have saved her from being crushed.

Mortimer Adler and Charles Van Doren write that "even in high tragedy . . . terrible things happen to good men, but we see that the hero, even if he does not wholly deserve his fate, at least comes to understand it" (221). Gertie's depth of understanding is ultimately what makes *The Dollmaker* so powerful. She learns to accept that her remaining children will slowly adjust to life in Detroit and become as foreigners to herself; she learns to accept that she can't hide from life.

In the final scene of the book, Gertie takes the one thing she has left that is truly hers — the block of wood she has been carving into a Christ figure — and takes an axe to it. She does what she has to do for her family's sake, and she does it freely. No one makes her do it. The face of Christ she had yearned to see in the block of wood would never materialize there. She has come to accept that she must seek Christ's face in the faces of her neighbors. And Gertie is right: no material happiness can save her or us. It is not in the materialization of even our most deeply held dreams but in serving the people around us that any of us ever sees the face of Christ.

Works Cited[2]

Adler, Mortimer, and Charles Van Doren. *How to Read a Book*. New York: Simon & Schuster, 1972.

Arnow, Harriet. *The Dollmaker*. New York: Avon Books, 1954.

---

[2] Normally, the Works Cited page would be on a separate sheet of paper; also, note that this sample essay was not double-spaced, nor did it have the appropriate header.

Literary Analysis Rubric

Criteria	Unacceptable	Acceptable	Excellent
Introduction Content	No author or title appears in the introduction; the writer makes no specific claim about the literary work nor narrows the focus to a specific aspect of it	The writer names the author and title of literary work(s) being analyzed and announces an intention to explore the work; however, the writer's focus may not be clear	The writer names the author and title of work(s) being analyzed and makes a specific claim or expresses a specific question about the literary work(s) in question
Authoritative Support	The writer does not support his or her ideas with evidence from the text	The writer supports assertions with summary, paraphrase, and quotations; however, quotations could be shorter, condensed, or integrated more smoothly	The writer supports assertions with ample evidence from the text, preferring summary and paraphrase and integrating quotations judiciously and smoothly
Correct Citations	The writer fails to include source information or page numbers for quoted material or includes no bibliography	The writer includes source information and page numbers for quoted material; however, the citations or entries in the bibliography contain formatting errors	The writer includes source information and a page number for all quoted material; the bibliography is correctly formatted and contains no errors
Clarity: Subjects and Verbs; Sentence correctness	Some sentences run on or are incomplete; sentences contain more than 5 errors in spelling, capitalization, or punctuation; 5 or more verbs per page are weak or nondescript	Sentences are complete and contain no more than 3 errors per page, subjects and verbs are generally clear, with fewer than 3 instances of passive voice or expletive construction, or weak or nondescript verbs per page	Sentences are complete and correct; the writer prefers to write with clear subjects and active verbs and can justify any use of the passive voice or expletive construction; no verbs are weak or nondescript
Coherence: Thoroughness and Order of Support	Sentences reflect no primary logical order; appear to be out-of-order or off-topic, and/or include logical gaps or redundancies	Sentences reflect a logical order and establish new ideas; any gap or overlap of ideas is slight	Sentences occur in a logical order and establish new ideas, and the writer interrupts this progression only to clarify or qualify points when necessary
Eloquence: Sentence length, type, and endings	Sentences include grammatically awkward structures, use sentence patterns repetitively, or fail to vary in length or type; concluding words lack emphasis or significance	Sentence length is mostly long; sentences do not repeat the same patterns; concluding statements emphasize final words	Sentence length is mostly long and reflect a variety of sentence structures; parallel structures are well-balanced; a few pithy statements are intriguing or powerful

```
Chapter 11
```

Research Papers

I still remember the day my husband told our family that he thought that the 1969 moon landing was either made up or exaggerated by the United States government. "Think about it," he said as we ate dinner that night. "It's 2009. The technology available to us now is not even comparable to the technology they had in 1969. It should be much cheaper, easier, and safer to explore space now than then. So why haven't we been back to the moon in decades?"

The idea struck us all as truly bizarre. We'd read about Apollo 11 in our history books and seen clips of it on TV. That it might have been faked seemed like an outrageous idea. But when my husband added the opinion that Nixon probably wasn't above using a television studio to fool the public into believing that America had made it to the moon under his administration, we couldn't help but admit, he had a point. (There aren't many politicians I'd trust much farther than I could throw a gum wrapper.) Suddenly, my husband's reasoning seemed plausible. Weird . . . but plausible.

At the time, Kristen was studying astronomy and theoretical physics, and her father's theory intrigued her. She decided to make the moon hoax theory her research project and determined to learn enough physics and astronomy to understand the issues involved in the various theories to weigh the evidence and come up with her own conclusion. Bizarre though it was, the moon hoax theory actually did seem to have a few things going for it, and Kristen really wanted to know if any of them held up under scrutiny.

POSING A QUESTION

Having a question students really want to know the answer to—or, at least, as close to an answer as possible—is the key to a good research paper. But not just any question will do. Too broad or speculative a question can lead to way too much research but no useful conclusions; too narrow a question can be sort of like painting yourself into a corner, leaving little or no room to explore. Hacker (2004) asserts that the best research questions are focused, thought-provoking, and grounded in facts, not speculation (p. 372-373). Taking the moon landing question as an example, consider each of the following potential questions:

Might the 1969 moon landing be a hoax?

This question is too speculative. It asks about possibilities, not facts. Heck, the Russians might have staged the moon landing themselves to make us think that they thought that we were beating them in the space race when in fact they knew that it was all a bit fat lie . . . but that, of course, would just be speculation. A better question would rely more on facts.

What reasons might the U.S. Government have had for faking the moon landing?

Again, this question is too speculative.

What are the various arguments against the 1969 moon landing?

This question is too broad: there are a surprising number of arguments that contend that 1969 moon landing was faked. Describing them all would feel more like an exercise in cataloging than determining the best possible conclusion to a serious question.

What obstacles would have had to be overcome in order to land human astronauts on the moon and was the technology available in 1969 adequate to those challenges?

This two-part question is too broad and probably too technical for most people to answer at all, much less for a high school student to tackle in ten to twenty pages.

Does the evidence support the theory that the 1969 moon landing was a hoax?

Bingo: this is a question that narrows the topic and defines the task; a student could feasibly conduct research on this topic, critically consider the evidence, and draw a conclusion that answers this question.

IDENTIFYING APPROPRIATE SOURCES

For a high school level research project, an appropriate minimum number of sources is five, including at least one electronic and one print source to familiarize students with both types of sources. Since the point of high school students writing a research project is less about contributing to a scholarly discussion than learning the process of gathering information from multiple sources, organizing that information into a coherent discussion, and drawing sound conclusions, it is not necessary to require purely academic or scholarly sources; however, students should understand that not all sources are equal.

Students should know whether their information constitutes an undisputed fact, a generally accepted theory, an expert opinion from someone who's either conducted studies or who discusses scholarly findings in writing, a popular opinion, or some kind of propaganda. Students should also be aware that many kinds of information can be written so as to mislead. For instance, just this week, I read a statistic that suggested that the majority of people believed something that I would consider fairly extreme. The statistic really surprised me until I noticed in the fine print that the survey had been conducted on a college campus known for its liberal values. That students on that college campus held the opinion did not surprise me in the least.

So almost any source may be biased or reliable; what's important is that students consider whether their information is likely to be reliable for their purposes based on where it's coming from. For instance, a student researching different makes of cars in order to decide which would be the best value could certainly use a manufacturer's website to verify facts such as what features a particular model has. On the other hand, the student should probably not consider the manufacturer as particularly credible source for the purpose of evaluation: obviously, Ford is going to say the Focus is the best small car on the market.

KEEPING TRACK OF INFORMATION AND SOURCES

Once upon a time, research papers required going to the library, taking extensive notes, and documenting source information meticulously. Thanks to the electronic age, the note card method is pretty much a thing of the past. While researching, students can track potentially pertinent information in print sources by using Post-it flags or page markers on useful passages and, with electronic sources, students can bookmark webpages or even copy and paste useful excerpts right into word processing documents along with a URL so they can relocate the source later if they decide to use the excerpt. Of course, students probably won't incorporate every source they peruse, and since they need to cite only the sources they actually use, all they need is to be able to relocate source information later.

ORGANIZING THE PAPER

After students have a good idea what their position about their topic will be, writing the paper is mostly a matter of organizing support, which will be easiest to do if students start with a hypothesis that answers the question that intrigued them in the first place. That hypothesis then becomes the thesis statement that determines the rest of the paper's organization. Far more so than the five-paragraph essays students have composed thus far, this composition will require students to determine an appropriate strategy for organizing the points they want to make. The argument form described in Chapter 9 can help students organize their ideas, and by thinking in terms of five sections (introduction, background information, argument 1, argument 2, and conclusion) rather than in trying to organize or outline an entire paper, students may feel less overwhelmed by the project's length.

WRITING THE PAPER

Remind students that the composition process for these essays is essentially the same as the one they have used previously: students devise their own thesis statements and make their own assertions. Paragraphs develop as in any other coherent progression, and students should interrupt this progression only to note that an idea or piece of information came from another source. If they can't remember where they found the material, they can simply writing '(source?)' to remind themselves to figure out which source to cite later. Postponing the chore of filling all of the source information allows students to focus on developing paragraphs, which really is the primary task.

It is a mistake to try to compose a research paper by piecing together the ideas of other writers. Students who try to simultaneously do research and write a research paper tend not to develop their own ideas on the topic but rather get bogged down with trying to accommodate the purposes of other writers—a more or less impossible challenge. Writing a research paper is much easier when students conduct research first, get a good sense of what they want to discuss in the paper, and only then write it. Students should rely mainly on what they have learned about their topic to inform their discussion and pull out a resource to consult, clarify a point, or quote only occasionally.

After writing the paper, students will need to fill in all of the missing source information. If students flagged sources with post-it notes or bookmarked them during the research stage, these should not be difficult to locate and cite. To format in-text citations and bibliographies correctly, students will need to consult a resource that shows how to format each of the myriad variations on how to cite different types of sources such as books with one, two, or more authors; books versus articles or websites; books that are edited, translated, or accessed online; journal or magazine articles; and the list goes on. I've listed a number of helpful sources for this, including a few that are available for free online, in Appendix A.

CITING SOURCES IN RESEARCH PAPERS

As with the literary analysis, the better part of what students incorporate from other authors should be summarized or paraphrased, and if students compose papers as described above, that's what will happen. Only occasionally should students use another author's exact wording in their research paper or argument.

Incorporating Summary and Paraphrase

A signal phrase tells readers that a particular idea or piece of information comes from another source, allowing students to give authors credit for their perspectives or research:

> **According to Mary Smith, as many as 38% of all Americans do not believe that the 1969 moon landing actually occurred.[3]**

Signal phrases also provide a subtle way for students to let their reader know that, while a perspective exists, they themselves don't necessarily agree:

> **Joe Smith suggests that the 1969 moon landing did not really happen because the technology to fake it existed at that time.**

These examples demonstrate two strategies for composing a signal phrase. The first incorporates the source's name into the beginning of the sentence and turn the main part of the sentence, the summary or paraphrase, into a dependent clause:

> **Mary Smith claims that as many as 38% of all Americans don't believe . . .**

> **Joe Smith suggests that the moon landing did not occur because . . . .**

This signal phrase requires an apt verb to describe what the author is doing in the quote. Does the author *claim, argue, assert, emphasize,* or *contend* a point, or does the author *describe, observe, state,* or *discuss* it? Maybe the author is less certain and only *notes, implies,* or *suggests*. Students might use other verbs in their signal phrases, but these are among the most useful.

A second signal phrase strategy calls for an introductory phrase that includes the author's name and expresses the main idea in the main sentence:

> **According to Mary Smith, [summarize, paraphrase or quote Smith here] (p. 150).**

> **In the words of Joe Smith, [quote Smith here] (150).**

---

[3] The sources and sample sentences on this and the next page are invented.

Notice the page number at the end of these examples. The exact formatting differs between documentation styles—that is, the 'p.' is correct for APA formatting, while just the page number is appropriate for MLA; either way, it is correct to tell your reader where to find the referred to information.

The first time an authoritative source is introduced in a paper, students should use a signal phrase and, if possible, identify the author's expertise: "According to psychologist Ron Brown . . ." In subsequent citations—or if the expertise of the author is not essential to the argument—students should simply note the author's last name in parentheses along with the page number after any summary or paraphrase to prevent cluttering the paper with excessive signal phrases:

> **As many as 38% of all Americans do not believe that the 1969 moon landing actually occurred (Smith 150).**

Since students lack the expertise to convince an audience, pointing to an authoritative source improves the credibility of their argument or discussion. In general, students should not rely on a quotation to make assertions; rather quotations should back up the students' assertions. When students use someone else's words to express their points, the paper feels cut-and-pasted, lacking in eloquence and often coherence as well.

That is why students should get in the habit of using what some people call a 'quote sandwich.' Just as a sandwich has three layers consisting of two pieces of bread on the outside and some substance in the middle, in a quote sandwich, the substance—the authoritative quote—is surrounded by the student's expression of an idea and the student's explanation or justification for including the quotation in his or her discussion:

Writer's assertion	**Teachers provide competent guidance and meaningful practice by planning instruction that gets students reading, writing, thinking, and discussing in order to achieve specific objectives.**
Signal phrase, quotation, And citation	**As Tyler (1949) puts it, "a student must have experiences that give him an opportunity to practice the kind of behavior implied by the objective" (p. 65).**
Writer's clarification	**That means that the teacher doesn't spend the bulk of class talking about reading, writing, thinking, and discussing. Rather, the teacher sets up situations so that students are challenged to do language arts themselves in authentic and meaningful ways.**

Incorporating Another Author's Words

Students should quote sources in an argument or research paper when an author's expertise lends authority to a point that the student wants to make or when an author's wording captures an idea so succinctly or eloquently that any paraphrase would only be wordy or awkward. Thus, students incorporate another author's words right into their own discussions when eloquence or precision of thought allows them to do so seamlessly:

> **Understanding any work of literature requires the student to "grasp the unity of the whole work" and to understand that "the unity of a story is always in its plot" (Adler & Van Doren, 1972, p. 209).**

Notice that the incorporated wording here is not a complete sentence but only a couple of phrases. It is a common error of students to incorporate too many of another author's words into their papers, effectively diluting their effect.

How can you tell if your student has incorporated an author's words into his or her paper appropriately? Compare the number of statistically improbable terms or word combinations in the quotations they've incorporated against the common, run-of-the-mill ones. If the quotation contains more common words and phrases than unusual, specific-to-the-topic-at-hand ones, then your student should either convey more of the idea in his or her own words and eliminate all but the essential heart of the quotation or, if the quotation has no essential core of meaning at all, he or she should probably just paraphrase the whole thing.

Long Quotations

Long quotations (four lines of text in MLA or forty words in APA) are more like a tostada than a sandwich—like a tostada, a largish pile of stuff rests on a sturdy but relatively thin foundation, which is the student's introduction. This introduction will be a complete sentence, which consists of a signal phrase and a brief summary of the author's take on things, usually ending with a colon.

> **The Anti-Federalists argue that granting unlimited powers to the national government necessarily abolishes American liberty. Even worse, the Anti-Federalists suspect that the prize for which the Federalists are willing to sacrifice liberty is national glory, a prize the Anti-Federalist Brutus rejects:**
>
> > **Let the monarchs, in Europe, share among them the glory of depopulating countries, and butchering thousands of their innocent**

> citizens, to revenge private quarrels, or to punish an insult offered
> to a wife, a mistress, or a favorite: I envy them not the honor, and I
> pray heaven this country may never be ambitious of it . . . The
> happiness of a people depends infinitely more on [the preservation
> of internal peace and good order] than it does upon all that glory
> and respect which nations acquire by the most brilliant martial
> achievements. (qtd. in Storing)

Assuming the long quote fits the purpose of the paper, no explanation is needed to cap it off; the student can move on to the next point in the paper. Students using long quotations—again, these should be infrequent—should follow the applicable formatting guidelines, omitting quotation marks and setting off the long quotation in a block as above.

General Knowledge

General knowledge doesn't need to be cited in a paper, but sometimes, it's hard to know what's considered general knowledge. One way to be reasonably sure is to consult a basic textbook for the subject within which the topic falls. If the information can be found in the textbook, it's general knowledge. Of course, students do need to cite a source when quoting a textbook's exact wording; however, in most cases, they would be better off to simply summarize the information.

FORMATTING THE PAPER AND BIBLIOGRAPHY

Both the bibliography, which is a list of the sources used in an academic paper, and the basic formatting for the paper, that is, the margins, line spacing, headers, page numbering, and headings, should conform to whatever system of documentation you require for your student. I recommend MLA for high school students because there is a decent chance that it is the style they will be required to use in college; also, of common documentation styles, I find it the least tedious to learn.

SAMPLE RESEARCH PAPER

This sample essay includes a number of characteristics you would expect to see in a research paper: appropriate formatting, a subtle thesis statement, background information defining the topic, section headings, a discussion of both sides of the issue, summaries, paraphrases, and quotations from authoritative sources, citations in the text, a conclusion based on the discussion of the topic, and a bibliography at the end.

Dena Luchsinger

Ms. Bauer

Advanced Composition

3 February 2012

Conspiracy Theorists:

Harmlessly Misguided or Dangerously Deluded?

Who's in control, and what are they doing to us? The popular 1999 movie, *The Matrix*, suggests the possibility of a world in which we only imagine the reality of our lives as we perceive them, when in truth we are all being held captive, hooked up to a giant system powered by our brain energy. In the movie, only a few worthy people are chosen to have this truth divulged to them so that they can fight against the evil conspiracy. In a humorous take on the same theme, the 1997 movie *Men in Black* describes a world in which aliens regularly appear on Earth, and FBI-like men wearing black secretly monitor alien activities and keep the aliens in line. In a kind of benevolent conspiracy, they erase the memories of normal people who learn too much. But the conspiracy theory movie that made the greatest impact on the American public was the 1991 film *JFK*, which reawakened curiosity about what really happened when President John F. Kennedy was shot. The movie expounded the position that Kennedy's assassination could not have been the work of a single man and that a conspiracy, potentially involving high officials and politicians in power at that time, was involved.

Although conspiracy theories had been around for centuries, *JFK* opened a conspiracy theory can of worms in America. For the past twenty years, financial insecurity combined with a deep distrust of government has spurred hundreds of conspiracy theories into being, and the Internet has provided a convenient medium for their dissemination. But what kind of people believe in these conspiracy theories, and are they always wrong to do so?

What is a Conspiracy Theory?

According to Wikipedia, "a conspiracy theory explains an event as being the result of an alleged plot by a covert group or organization or, more broadly, the idea that important political, social or economic events are the products of secret plots that are largely unknown to the general public." Another definition states that a conspiracy theory is "an effort to explain some event or practice by reference to the machinations of powerful people who have also managed to conceal their role" (Sunstein & Vermeule 4). People who generate and believe conspiracy theories tend to be intuitive transcendentalists who believe that everything that happens is interconnected and that everything happens for a reason: "Conspiracy theories connect the dots of random events into meaningful patterns and then infuse those patterns with intentional agency" (Shermer).

Once a person accepts a theory that fits the person's ideas about what happened, the person can rarely be dissuaded, even by objective evidence that effectively disproves the theory. In fact, because the nature of conspiracy is secrecy, believers are inclined to consider anything that opposes their belief as proof that they're right and the conspirators, who don't want to be exposed, are spreading disinformation to throw them off their scent. This is because conspiracy theories, as Law professors Cass Sunstein and Adrian Vermeuele explain, "have a self-sealing quality, rendering them particularly immune to challenge" (3).

Michael Shermer recounts a conversation he had in 2005, when he was approached by someone who believed that 9/11 was really the result of a conspiracy within our own government. "But didn't Osama and some members of al Qaeda not only say they did it, they gloated about what a glorious triumph it was?" Shermer asked. Not to be deterred, the man had an explanation for the video of bin Laden: "That's what they want you to believe," the man said. "That was faked by the CIA and leaked to the press to mislead us" (qtd. in Shermer). Because the man believed that the government was behind 9/11, any evidence to the contrary only reinforced his believe that "they" were trying to cover it up.

Why People Believe Conspiracy Theories

Conspiracy theories are sometimes the product of mental illness. For instance, Nobel prize-winning mathematician John Nash developed a belief in conspiracy theories as a symptom of schizophrenia. In her biography of Nash, Sylvia Nasar describes Nash's delusions. In one of the first incidents, Nash walked into a common room holding a newspaper and said that "abstract powers from outer space or perhaps it was foreign governments, were communicating with him through the New York Times. The messages, which were meant only for him, were encrypted and required close analysis" (241). Soon Nash began to notice patterns in neckties and in radio transmissions as well, and he became obsessed with understanding the messages. His wife and friends realized that he was suffering delusions and sought help. Later, when asked by a former colleague how a mathematician devoted to reason and logical proof could have believed that extraterrestrials were sending him messages, Nash answered, "The ideas I had about supernatural beings came to me the same way my mathematical ideas did. So I took them seriously" (11).

Although some conspiracy theories are caused by mental illnesses such as schizophrenia or paranoia, most of these conspiracy theories are isolated; they have nothing to do with the widespread conspiracy theories that proliferate on the Internet today. As Sunstein and Vermeule point out, "it is not plausible to suggest that all or most members of those communities are afflicted by mental illness" (9). Rather, the typical conspiracy theory circulating today proliferates as a result of two phenomena: modern technology (Harding 1) and what Sunstein and Vermeule term 'crippled epistemologies' (8).

Nick Harding asserts that the Internet is largely to blame. He contrasts the years it used to take to formulate and disseminate conspiracy theories with today: "social networking sites allow conspiracy theorists to seek out and link with like-minded individuals . . . . people interested in conspiracy also have access to vast online depositories of reference material which can be selectively edited to support an idea" (2). Because social networking sites and YouTube sites attract mainly younger viewers, many teenagers and young adults accept conspiracy theories without really thinking about them or asking what evidence there is for accepting the theory.

This is what Sunstein and Vermeuele mean when they say that most of the people who believe in conspiracy theories "suffer from a 'crippled epistemology,' in the sense that they know very few things, and what they know is wrong" (9). For example, take the idea that that NASA and government officials conspired to fake the 1969 moon landing. For the most part, the people who conjecture that the moon landing was faked have very limited direct knowledge about astronomy or rocketry; their knowledge is generally based on the opinions of other people, and their conclusions may be based on faulty understandings of science. Of course, they may still be right in their conclusions—but to date, the hard evidence justifying that position has not come to light.

Psychologist Ted Goertzel notes that people most likely to believe in conspiracy theories hold a minority status, believe that things are getting worse in general, and feel they cannot trust "the police, their neighbors, or their relatives" (6). Analyzing results further, Goertzel discovered that "age and economic security were not statistically significant" (7). Another psychologist, Douglas Kenrick, however, writes that "conspiracy beliefs have been linked to being poor, being a member of a downtrodden minority, having a general sense that one's life is controlled by external factors, and other unfortunate circumstances" (1).

That economically disadvantaged minorities who feel beaten down by the system would accept conspiracy theories more than other people makes sense, considering that what such people know for a fact is that the system has not worked in their favor. What's more, such people often find themselves the victims of government bureaucracy, which often involves a lot of hassle and frustration. People who have to work with government agencies to get what they need often conclude that the system either doesn't care about them or is actively against them.

Most people have only very vague ideas about how abstract categories of reality like 'government' or even subsidiaries thereof, like the 'IRS,' really work. Most people don't realize that bureaucracy is essentially a factory in which tasks are divvied out to maximize production, the only difference being the "arbitrariness by which bureaucratic processes are superimposed" (Berger, Berger, & Kellner 42). What people do know is that "each agency . . . [has] expert knowledge appropriate to this sphere [of life]" (Berger, Berger, & Kellner 43) and that "the bureaucrat is not concerned with the individual in the flesh before him but with his 'file'" (Berger, Berger, & Kellner 47). These understandings lead people who have dealings with any government bureaucracy to conclude that critical information is being withheld from them and that the people on the other side of the desk are not on their side.

Since a bureaucracy does not actually produce anything, its goal is always to simply run smoothly. When anyone complains or presents a problem, legitimate or otherwise, some bureaucrat has to deal with it. Bureaucrats exist to make problems go away. As a result, an individual person who confronts a government bureaucrat may conclude that an unnamed "they" is trying to defeat them. And, in a sense, "they" is—only "they" in this case is bureaucracy itself, which exists to run and, in theory, serve people as efficiently as possible. However, this unnamed "they" is not any particular person or group of people; there is no conspiracy, just bureaucracy.

When Conspiracies are Real

That is not to say that conspiracies don't exist within government agencies, because they do. The famous example of Watergate is described in detail in Carl Bernstein and Bob Woodward's book, *All the President's Men*, which describes the conspiracy of President Richard Nixon and several members of his staff who sabotaged an opponent's political campaign and then committed perjury to cover it up. Although initially, relatively few people knew of the plan to break into the Watergate Hotel, the web of lies and cover-up involved so many people so that, eventually, someone in the know felt compelled to leak the truth. And, of course, that is exactly what happened: an associate director of the FBI assumed the pseudonym Deep Throat and gradually revealed enough about the scandal for investigative reporters Bernstein and Woodward to discover the truth.

The problem with many of the most absurd and dangerous conspiracy theories is that they require cascade logic, or "reasoning that requires believers to implicate more and more people in the conspiracy whenever anyone reports evidence against their claims" (Kenrick 2). Believers in conspiracy theories grossly "overestimate the competence and discretion of officials and bureaucracies" (Sunstein & Vermeule 7). Realistically, in an open society with a free press, government officials just aren't going to be able to coordinate and carry out nefarious plans without someone on the outside finding out about it or someone on the inside leaking it to the press.

Dan O'Neill's book *The Firecracker Boys* recounts the story of a real government conspiracy that was actually debunked in time to prevent a hideous plan from being carried out. The book details government plans to detonate thermonuclear bombs thirty miles from a settlement of native Alaskans. The project, deemed Project Chariot, was proposed by the Atomic Energy Commission (AEC), whose mission was to develop peace-time applications for nuclear weapons. Because the AEC dealt with nuclear weaponry, it was permitted to operate with a high degree of secrecy that prohibited outsiders from gaining access to information that would allow them to scrutinize planned projects and consider whether these might hold implications for public health and safety (16). When officials of AEC explained the plan to carve out a harbor in Northern Alaska using several thermonuclear bombs, they emphasized that the plan "would be conducted only if [preliminary] studies showed that the project would be safe" (170). Originally hyped for its economic advantages to Alaska, AEC did not scrap the project when Alaskan legislators and businessmen lacked enthusiasm for the prospect of a harbor which would be ice-locked the better part of the year and so far from natural resources as to be virtually useless (36). Nevertheless, the project was not scrapped. Later, during a goodwill visit to the Inupiat community situated nearest to the proposed detonation site, AEC officials knowingly misinformed the villagers, saying that

> the nuclear tests at the Pacific Proving Grounds had not contaminated fish with radiation such that the fish were unfit to eat; that radioactive fallout from the [intended] blast would be so little that it would probably not be measurable with radiation detection equipment; that the harmful constituents of fallout would for the most part be gone from Ogotoruk Creek in a matter of hours; that people at Point Hope would not feel the seismic shock of the Chariot detonation thirty-one miles away; that a study of cattle in the Nevada desert offered evidence as to the harmlessness of fallout moving through an Arctic ecosystem; that American nuclear testing had not harmed 'Indian' people anywhere; and that once Japanese who received 'very great exposures' recovered from radiation sickness, they suffered no further effects. (141)

The AEC representatives expected the villagers of Point Hope to be ignorant dupes, but in fact they were quite knowledgeable about the dangers of nuclear fallout, and they opposed the plan unanimously. Meanwhile, the AEC representatives continuously bungled their roles. They not only offended the villagers at Point Hope by laughing at their concerns, but they galvanized the academic community at University of Alaska at Fairbanks by publishing a report that falsified data gathered by University biologists hired to assess the advisability of the project, slanting the results to favor the project (204).

About that time, people began to realize that the AEC intended to detonate the bombs whether the detonation were deemed safe or not, and several individuals began to publicize their concerns—and encounter opposition. Don Foote, a geographer hired to do topography and soil studies near the site, began to suspect that he was being followed after he began to oppose the project, writing in a letter to a friend that "The Alaska Chariot scene is boiling . . . Have reason to believe an FBI or CIA agent is on my track" (221). Foote's friend wired back to confirm his suspicion.

Still, too many people had realized that the AEC was up to no good, and they began to publicize their reasons for believing so. Eventually, their efforts made public headlines and attracted the attention of Washington officials who began to withdraw their support for the project. Finally, after a harrowing and high-stakes conflict, Sharon Francis, a sympathizer who worked in the Department of the Interior in Washington D.C., was able to write to Don Foote that the AEC, "rather than have [the Office of the Interior] issue a counter-report to the President which . . . would have been most embarrassing to the AEC, they withdrew early in the fray, and in the most face-saving manner" (qtd. in O'Neill 277).

Conclusions

Rock star Kurt Cobain once said, "Just because you're paranoid don't mean they're not after you." Cobain was only partly right; it would be more true to say that just because conspiracies do exist doesn't mean that you're on to one.

Factual evidence, first-hand knowledge, and logical processes are the key to defeating real conspiracies and debunking fake ones. Goertzel points out that productive conspiracy thinkers "develop highly idiosyncratic theories and gather evidence to test them" (13). They "engage in a dialogue with their context" and accept that a theory may be disproved by new evidence about it (12).

Conspiracy theories can be intriguing, and certainly some conspiracy theories are essentially harmless. Sunstein and Vermeuele point out that to children, the whole Tooth Fairy thing is a conspiracy in which powerful people—in this case, parents—mislead their constituents—i.e., their children—into believing that the Tooth Fairy exists (5). Many if not most popular conspiracy theories, however, are not harmless: not only do they undermine what little trust people have in the goodness of genuinely earnest people who happen to work in government agencies, they train people to think irrationally. According to psychology professor Chris Finch, "The single greatest predictor of whether you believe in a conspiracy theory is whether you believe in other conspiracy theories, even when there is no connection [between them]" (qtd. in Harding 3).

People who buy into conspiracy theories learn to accept that evidence that disproves a position must actually prove it. Such logic will not help people achieve their ends in the real world. On the contrary, people who believe in conspiracy theories become mired in irrational thinking strategies that decrease their ability to be heard and respected by other people. Thus it is not conspiracy theories themselves, but the kind of thinking that accompanies false theories that must be combated.

Works Cited[4]

Berger, Peter, Brigitte Berger, and Hansfried Kellner. *The Homeless Mind:*
    Modernization and Consciousness. New York: Vintage Books, 1973. Print.

"Conspiracy Theory." *Wikipedia.* Wikipedia Foundation. 16 Feb. 2012 Web. 17 Feb.
    2012

Goertzel, Ted. "Belief in Conspiracy Theories." *Political Psychology* 15 (1994): n.pag.
    Web. 17 Feb. 2012.

Harding, Nick. "Truth and Lies: Conspiracy Theories are Running Rampant Thanks
    to Modern Technology." *Independent.co.uk.* The Independent, 12 Nov. 2011
    Web. 17 Feb. 2012.

Kenrick, Douglas. "Why the Human Brain is Designed to Distrust." *Psychology*
    Today.com. Sussex Publishers, 15 July 2011. Web. 17 Feb. 2012.

O'Neill, Dan. *The Firecracker Boys: H-Bombs, Inupiat Eskimos, and the Roots of the*
    Environmental Movement. Philadelphia, PA: Basic Books, 1994. Print.

Nasar, Sylvia. *A Beautiful Mind.* New York: Touchstone, 1998. Print.

Shermer, Michael. "Why People Believe in Conspiracies." *ScientificAmerican.com.*
    Scientific American, 10 Sept. 2009. Web. 17 Feb. 2012.

Sunstein, Cass and Adrian Vermeule. "Conspiracy Theories." 15 January 2008. Web.
    PDF file.

---

[4] Normally, the Works Cited page would be on a separate sheet of paper; also, note that this sample essay was not double-spaced, nor did it have the appropriate MLA header.

Research Paper Rubric

Criteria	Unacceptable	Acceptable	Excellent
Topic and Content	The writer chooses an issue that involves no controversy or addresses questions that are too broad or narrow to arrive at a helpful conclusion	The writer begins with a controversial question and discusses at least two sides of the issue, but the discussion is either weak on one side or does not lead to any real conclusion	The writer begins with a controversial question that is neither too broad nor too narrow and discusses at least two sides of the issue in order to arrive at a reasonable conclusion
Organization	The organization of ideas is not clear to readers; no sections are clear; any conclusion seems premature or poorly supported	The writer uses an outline to organize ideas, but paragraphs switch between topics or perspectives too frequently; the progression feels jerky to the reader	The writer uses the argument form to organize ideas effectively and lead to a conclusion
Authoritative Support	Authoritative support is scant or inappropriately cited; references include several errors (4 or more omissions or formatting errors)	Authoritative support is appropriately cited in two out of three body paragraphs; references are complete and mostly correct (3 or fewer errors)	Authoritative support is evident and appropriately cited in all body paragraphs; references are complete and correctly formatted both in the text and in the bibliography
Clarity	Some sentences run on or are incomplete; sentences contain more than 5 errors in spelling, capitalization, or punctuation; 5 or more verbs per page are weak or nondescript	Sentences are complete and contain no more than 3 errors per page, subjects and verbs are generally clear, with fewer than 3 instances of passive voice or expletive construction, or weak or nondescript verbs per page	Sentences are complete and correct; the writer prefers to write with clear subjects and active verbs and can justify any use of the passive voice or expletive construction; no verbs are weak or nondescript
Coherence	Sentences reflect no primary logical order; some sentences appear to be out-of-order or off-topic, and/or include logical gaps or redundancies	Sentences reflect a logical order and establish new ideas; any gap or overlap of ideas is slight	Sentences occur in a logical order and establish new ideas, and the writer interrupts this progression only to clarify or qualify points when necessary
Eloquence	Sentences include grammatically awkward structures, use sentence patterns repetitively, or fail to vary in length or type; concluding words lack emphasis or significance	Sentence length is mostly long; sentences do not repeat the same patterns; concluding statements emphasize final words	Sentence length is mostly long and reflects a variety of sentence structures; parallel structures are well-balanced; a few pithy statements are intriguing or powerful

Research Paper Checklist

Topic

- ☐ Does the student begin with a question to which he or she wants an answer?
- ☐ Does the question define the research topic without being too speculative?
- ☐ Does the topic involve some degree of controversy or disagreement; i.e., does it allow for real discussion?

Content

- ☐ Does the student develop his or her own discussion and use quotations only for authoritative evidence or support?
- ☐ Does the student give equal consideration to each perspective on the topic?
- ☐ Does the student incorporate authoritative quotations into his or her argument or discussion with discretion and precision?

Sources

- ☐ Does the student cite at least five sources in his or her paper?
- ☐ Are sources appropriate to purposes—that is, are authoritative quotations from reliable sources or experts rather than uninformed or biased people?

Citations

- ☐ Does the student introduce sources with a signal phrase?
- ☐ Does the student "sandwich" quotations between an introductory summary and an explanatory note about the material's relevance?
- ☐ Does the student exclude impertinent material with ellipses?
- ☐ Does the student use brackets to clarify ambiguous quotes?
- ☐ Does the student cite the author and the page number (if available) for quoted material?

Documentation

- ☐ Does the student append a bibliography at the end of the paper?
- ☐ Does the student format the paper and bibliography appropriately for the documentation style employed?

Chapter 12

Researched Argument

The summer before her senior year of high school, Kristen told me that she had decided to become vegetarian. She had considered the idea for some time and was resolved. Now, I had advocated less meat and more beans for years as being both healthy and economical, but I had never considered eating no meat at all. I was afraid Kristen wouldn't get enough protein and possibly other nutrients as well. I knew she wouldn't die, but I had some serious concerns. I finally decided that I could support Kristen's decision, but only if she took responsibility for discovering what she needed to do to stay healthy without eating meat and wrote a paper to convince me that her decision was sound. Since vegetarianism had become important to Kristen, she willingly set about finding books and articles that would inform her position, and the paper she wrote was so effective that, to her delight and her father's chagrin, I began preparing meatless meals much more often.

Choosing topics that students really care about is the key to any argument. When high school students reach their junior and senior years, they often develop interests, hopes, and dreams about who they are and what their futures might be. Perhaps for the first time, their writing can serve an authentic purpose for them, because they can use it to convince you that they have thought deeply about important matters and carved out real understanding. Writing a researched argument, therefore, presents a purpose for writing that may well be the first that students truly care about. A researched argument is the perfect way for high school students to prove to their parents that their positions merit being taken seriously.

DEVISING A THESIS FOR AN ARGUMENT

An argument implies not only a persuasive purpose but also a well-researched and reasoned presentation of ideas. It resembles a research paper in that it requires research, but whereas in a research paper, students search for answers, in a researched argument, students have an answer already. The point of the argument is to convince an audience that their answer is the best one: "The purpose of argumentation within a free society," Richard

Fulkerson writes, "is to reach the best conclusion possible at the time" (as cited in Hacker, 2004, p. 344). The best presentation for an argument is the five-section argument form described in Chapter 9, which perfectly fits the purpose of convincing an audience of a position.

The thesis in an argument takes a very specific form: it announces a position, or what the student is arguing in the paper, and cites reasons for its acceptance. This thesis is actually fairly easy to write because it follows a simple formula: it starts by announcing the specific assertion about the topic that the student wants to argue, and it lists the best reasons for accepting the position as the most sensible one to take. The word 'because' serves as a kind of fulcrum for the two parts of the thesis.

> **A balanced vegetarian diet may be the healthiest choice because a variety of plant-based foods contains more diverse and abundant nutrients than the typical American meat-centered diet, many meat and dairy-heavy foods contain large quantities of fat which contribute to lethargy and obesity, and excessive animal protein promotes cancer and heart disease.**

Although this thesis statement seems complicated, you can see how the content of the thesis merely fills in the formula:

Formula for Argument-style Thesis

		First Reason for the Argument
What the Student has to say about the topic (i.e., the argument)	**BECAUSE**	Second Reason for the Argument
		Third Reason for the Argument

Of course, while this formula is trustworthy, structurally, it can be reversed to improve the flow of the introductory paragraph.

> **State and federal legislators should ban the use of hazardous wastes as ingredients in fertilizers because the toxic substances contaminate the environment and enter the food chain.**

Can also be written:

> **Because the toxic substances contaminate the environment and enter the food chain, state and federal legislators should ban the use of hazardous wastes as ingredients in fertilizers.**

Many arguments involve research topics, but arguments can also apply to a literary analysis as well. Here is an argument for an understanding of two literary characters:

> **Elizabeth Gaskell's character John Thornton strikes readers as more sympathetic than Jane Austen's Fitzwilliam Darcy because Darcy's initial attitudes about the lower classes offends readers while Thornton's attitudes about the classes are more realistic; Darcy inherits his wealth while Thornton works for his; and whereas Austen limits Darcy's perspective to one letter, Gaskell gives readers frequent insights into Thornton's thoughts and feelings.**

As you can see, the thesis statement in an argument can be quite extensive, but it need not be daunting, so long as writers recall the purpose of a thesis statement, which is to provide the reader an overview of the paper as a whole. Each of the reasons listed in the thesis is a main part of the argument which will serve as the topic sentence for one of the body paragraphs of the argument section of the paper.

Sources for the Researched Argument

As with any research paper, a researched argument requires adequate support from at least five reputable or authoritative sources. One distinction with a researched argument, however, is that the number of sources need not be equal for both sides of the argument. As you know, the argument form requires writers to acknowledge and refute the opposing perspective. If the student has selected reputable sources to support his or her position, those sources will probably contain refutations themselves, effectively informing the student about what opposition exists as well as what arguments serve to refute it. Nevertheless, students should seek out at least one source that represents the opposing viewpoint and seriously consider the author's point-of-view. Only after taking the opposition seriously can students respect the perspective and give it a fair rebuttal.

Documentation in a Researched Argument

The instructions for documenting sources in a research paper in the previous chapter apply to researched arguments as well. Here, I would address just one question that often arises with arguments: how to incorporate quotations from outside sources found within a document by another author. Say a student encounters the perfect quotation and wants to include it in his or her paper, but since the author of the quotation is not the author of the article or book that will be cited in the bibliography, the quotation may seem as if it were written by the wrong author. Happily, there is an easy fix for this: Simply identify the author of the quotation in a signal phrase and the author of the source where the quotation was found in the citation, using the phrase (as cited in Smith) for APA and (qtd. in Smith) for MLA.

> **Dick Camp, President of Bay Zinc, observes, "When it goes into the silo, it's a hazardous waste. When it comes out, it's no longer regulated. The exact same material" (qtd. in Wilson).**

Argument Rubric

For this essay, you have two choices: either combine criteria from previous levels, highlighting one or two specific goals your student continues to struggle with, or use the Researched Argument Rubric found on page 144.

SAMPLE RESEARCHED ARGUMENT

Dena Luchsinger

Ms. Bauer

Advanced Composition

22 March 2012

Recycling Gone Wrong:

Hazardous Waste in Fertilizer

Why did two prize-winning herds of dairy cows suddenly die by the hundreds? Why is lead being detected in fruits, grains, and vegetables? Why is production down by half or more on once productive farms? The answer, some say, lies in the currently legal practice of fertilizer companies using hazardous wastes as inert ingredient filler in their products. Since current regulations require fertilizer companies to list only the beneficial nutrients like nitrogen, phosphorus, and potassium, farmers and gardeners don't know that they are spreading toxins like arsenic, lead, and mercury on their land and in their gardens. Once employed, these heavy metals and toxic chemicals are impossible to remove from soil. Because the toxic substances contaminate the environment and enter the food chain, state and federal legislators should ban the use of hazardous wastes as ingredients in fertilizers.

Over the past thirty years, companies have been using the hazardous wastes produced from smelting, mining, burning medical and municipal wastes and other heavy industries as inert ingredients in fertilizer. Fertilizers sold for the beneficial nutrients and micronutrients such as nitrogen, phosphorus, potassium, zinc, calcium, and sulfur, all of which optimize plant growth, may contain industrial wastes like "plutonium, arsenic, mercury, cadmium, lead, PCBs and dioxin" (Rutter). Many critics feel that current regulations allow companies that produce industrial wastes to avoid the expense of disposing of waste properly and even profit by selling what is suddenly and inexplicably a valuable product: Dick Camp, President of Bay Zinc, observes, "When it goes into the silo, it's a hazardous waste. When it comes out, it's no longer regulated. The exact same material" (qtd. in Wilson).

Many of the heavy metals and chemicals found in hazardous materials have been linked to cancer and birth defects in humans. People may be exposed to hazardous wastes in fertilizers in several ways, including ingestion, inhalation, and absorption. Anyone whose skin touches a lawn, golf course, ball field, school yard, or park ground fertilized with toxic substances such as lead, cadmium, and mercury could suffer effects from "mild skin irritation" to "more serious problems like burns, sores, or ulcers on the outer layers of the skin" ("Hazardous Materials"). Children who spend a lot of time on the ground "are most susceptible to the toxic effects of most metals, especially lead" (Schaffer). Even trace amounts of lead can affect health, resulting in developmental problems (Wilson). One can also be contaminated by breathing toxic substances into the lungs, especially if a person lives near a contaminated area, such as a field ("Hazardous Materials").

Since plants absorb toxic substances from soil, people may also become ill after ingesting foods grown in contaminated soils. Root crops like carrots, onions, and potatoes, for instance, absorb arsenic from soil, while fruits and grains absorb lead (Shaffer). Environmental studies professor Adrienne Anderson discovered wheat crops "grown in sludge incorporating . . . plutonium and other wastes" were being sold as specialty baked goods, noting sardonically that the goods are indeed "special" (Rutter). Although few studies have been conducted to examine the effects of consuming food grown in soil fertilized by products including hazardous wastes, studies in Japan verified that people became sick after eating rice grown with fertilizer containing cadmium (Wilson).

Not only do hazardous wastes endanger people through immediate exposure, their application on farmland threatens future generations as well. In a letter to the editor, Professor Emeritus Caroline Snyder points out that, since farmers determine application rates by nitrogen levels and since Class A Biosolids contain little nitrogen, farmers may apply large amounts to fields, "until the treated land has been turned into a low-level hazardous waste site and yields reduced by 50 percent" (Snyder). She notes that a federal judge recently ordered the USDA to compensate one farmer whose land was "so poisoned by sludge that it was no longer capable of growing crops" (Snyder). Hazardous wastes such as lead, mercury, arsenic, cadmium, and dioxin found in fertilizers accumulate and persist in the soil, effectively destroying farmland forever (Shaffer).

Critics think that those who oppose the use of hazardous waste in fertilizer overstate their argument since the majority of fertilizer products are thought to be free of harmful levels of hazardous materials. Richard Koenig, an expert on soil fertility, estimates that no more than 5 – 10% of fertilizers are composed of hazardous waste derivatives (qtd. in Rutter). The Environmental Protection Agency regards the incorporation of hazardous wastes into fertilizer products as a "beneficial reuse and recycling of industrial wastes . . . when such wastes can be used as safe and effective substitutes for virgin raw materials" (EPA). EPA specifies safe concentration levels of heavy metals and toxic matter in fertilizers "based on the 'best demonstrated available technology'" (EPA). State agencies are then responsible for administering these federal regulations, some states being more stringent than others in their regulation. Koenig maintains that state and federal regulations adequately protect consumers, but believes that consumers ultimately bear the burden of determining the safety of fertilizer products before use (qtd. in Rutter).

Unfortunately, current laws require fertilizer companies to list only beneficial ingredients on labels; anyone who wants to know exactly what a particular fertilizer contains must submit samples of the fertilizer for testing or research products online. Consumers who are unaware that as many as one of every ten fertilizer products contains hazardous waste are unlikely to take precautions before spreading the material on fields, gardens, or lawns. Indeed, the fertilizer industry misleads consumers in its promotional literature, which describe immediate benefits of the beneficial ingredients of fertilizer and omit any mention of the synthetic chemicals and heavy metals that don't break down but do accumulate in the soil. Moreover, EPA's regulation extends to just eight toxic metals, when waste products are "such a complex and unpredictable mixture of [90,000] chemical compounds . . . that chemical-by-chemical risk assessment does not adequately protect human health" (Snyder).

Franklin D. Roosevelt once said, "A nation that destroys its soils destroys itself." Even if hazardous wastes make up some part of just 5 – 10% of the fertilizers used in America, that's still contaminating 5 – 10% too much of our country's farmable land. Other countries value their land too highly to risk destroying such a precious resource as their soil. It may be convenient for EPA to call it recycling, and it may be profitable for big businesses to unload their hazardous wastes on unsuspecting farmers, but destroying the land has implications for this and future generations. Our legislators, at both the state and federal levels, are charged with defending the rights of their constituents. The right to living in a land unspoiled by toxic contaminants is one all legislators should defend.

Works Cited[5]

Rutter, Diane O. "Gleanings: A Growing Concern: Hazardous Waste in Fertilizer." *The New Farm.* Rodale Institute. May 2003. Web. 12 Feb. 2012.

Shaffer, Matthew. "Waste Lands: The Threat of Toxic Fertilizer." *California Public Interest Research Group.* 2001. Web. 12 Feb. 2012.

Snyder, Caroline. "Biosolids are Not a Fertilizer." *FarmingMagazine.com.* June 2011. Moose River Media. Web. 12 Feb. 2012.

The State University of New Jersey, Rutgers. "Public Health Concerns with Hazardous Materials in Fertilizers." *The Soil Profile.* 16 (2006): n.pag. Web. 12 Feb. 2012. PDF file.

United States. Environmental Protection Agency. Office of Solid Waste. "Environmental Fact Sheet: Waste-Derived Fertilizers." EPA. December 1997. Web. 12 Feb. 2012. PDF file.

University of Nebraska at Omaha. "Hazardous Materials and Human Health." PDF file.

Wilson, Duff. "Killing Fields? Toxic Waste Being Spread as Fertilizer." Seattle Times. 5 July 1997. Web. 12 Feb. 2012.

---

[5] Normally, the Works Cited page would be on a separate sheet of paper; also, note that this sample essay was not double-spaced, nor did it have the appropriate header.

Researched Argument Rubric

Criteria	Unacceptable	Acceptable	Excellent
Topic and Content	The writer introduces a controversial topic, but fails to include background information, argue effectively, or refute the opposing perspective	The writer announces a position about a topic in a thesis statement and provides background information and an effective argument for the position	The writer engages the reader, introduces a controversial topic, and gives reasons for a position in a thesis statement in the introduction; the writer provides background information, argues effectively for the position, and refutes the opposition in the body, and reiterates the position and concludes eloquently
Organization	The organization of ideas is not clear to readers; any conclusion seems premature or poorly supported	The writer uses an outline to organize ideas, but order of paragraphs switches between topics or perspectives too frequently; feels jerky to the reader	The writer uses the argument form to organize ideas effectively and lead to a conclusion
Authoritative Support	Authoritative support is scant or inappropriately cited; references include several errors (5 or more omissions or formatting errors)	Authoritative support is appropriately cited in two out of three body paragraphs; references are complete and mostly correct (3 or fewer errors)	Authoritative support is evident and appropriately cited in all body paragraphs; references are complete and correctly formatted both in the text and in the bibliography
Clarity	Some sentences run on or are incomplete; sentences contain more than 5 errors in spelling, capitalization, or punctuation; 5 verbs are weak or nondescript	Sentences contain no more than 3 errors per page, subjects and verbs are generally clear, fewer than 3 weak or nondescript verbs appear per page	Complete, correct sentences contain clear subjects and active verbs; the writer can justify any use of the passive voice or expletive construction
Coherence	Sentences reflect no primary logical order; some sentences appear be out-of-order or off-topic, and/or include logical gaps or redundancies	Sentences reflect a logical order and establish new ideas; any gap or overlap of ideas is slight	Sentences occur in a logical order and establish new ideas, and the writer interrupts this progression only to clarify or qualify points when necessary
Eloquence	Sentences include grammatically awkward structures, use sentence patterns repetitively, or fail to vary in length or type; concluding words lack emphasis or significance	Sentence length is mostly long; sentences do not repeat the same patterns; concluding statements emphasize final words	Sentence length is mostly long and reflects a variety of sentence structures; parallel structures are well-balanced; a few pithy statements are intriguing or powerful

Researched Argument Checklist

Topic

☐ Does the topic intrigue or incite the student—does the student really care?

☐ Does the topic involve some degree of controversy or disagreement; i.e., is there any real opposition to the student's position that must be refuted?

Content

☐ Does the student develop his or her own argument and use quotations mainly for authoritative support?

☐ Does the student incorporate authoritative quotations into his or her argument with discretion and precision?

☐ Does the student primarily argue his or her position in the body?

☐ Does the student acknowledge and refute the opposing perspective?

Sources

☐ Does the student cite at least five outside sources in his or her paper?

☐ Does at least one source represent the opposition's perspective?

☐ Are sources appropriate to purposes—that is, are authoritative quotations from scholars or experts rather than strictly biased individuals?

Citations

☐ Does the student introduce sources with a signal phrase?

☐ Does the student exclude impertinent material with ellipses?

☐ Does the student use brackets to clarify ambiguous quotes?

☐ Does the student cite the author and the page number (if available) for quoted material?

Documentation

☐ Does the student append a bibliography at the end of the paper?

☐ Does the student format the paper and bibliography appropriately for the documentation style employed?

Addendum:

Alternate Purposes

&

Functional Communication

Chapter 13

Timed Essays

Two of the most stressful writing tasks many high school students face are college aptitude tests and graduation qualifying exams. Somewhat bizarrely, the kind of writing students need to do to do well on timed tests like these is completely unlike any of the writing they will have learned or will ever have to do again.

First, an essay written and submitted in less than an hour (often less) can only be called a first draft. A timed testing situation allows almost no time for planning, revising, or editing. Also, with no opportunity for research, students must rely on what they already know. As a result, support for these essays mostly comes from personal experiences and observations, although ideally these will be supplemented by some knowledge acquired in school. Because of this, most tests use prompts that force students to use illustrative examples to support their positions. A final oddity with high-stakes testing situations is that they require students to write with a pencil, which many students no longer do. Students who typically write essays using a computer may be surprised at the way their out-of-shape hand muscles scream at having to keep a pencil in motion for twenty-five to forty minutes straight. These students do well to practice writing several practice essays out by hand.

The academic prompt for this type of essay requires the student to make a decision on a controversial topic that does not have a single correct answer. Generally, these prompts present students with a dilemma that has moral or ethical implications upon which students must take a position; however, students should be aware that assessors are not looking for them to choose the "right" answer, but rather to provide solid reasoning for whichever position they take. Because the student's purpose in this essay is to persuade the reader to a particular position, he or she must provide thorough support for a clear and unambiguous answer.

Here is an example of a position paper designed for a state examination:

> Many professional athletes and celebrities, e.g., movie stars and musical recording artists, receive multimillion-dollar salaries. Many people believe these salaries are excessive; others believe they are justifiable. Write an editorial for your local newspaper in which you defend or oppose the salaries of athletes and/or celebrities. (Delaware State Department of Education 2000, as cited in Gere, Christenbury, & Sassi, 2005, p. 144)

The SAT prompt asks students to consider an excerpt before considering their response:

> Most people tend to trust others too readily. To avoid being taken advantage of, however, it is generally wise to be doubtful and suspicious of others' motives or honesty. Many people would agree that if you find yourself doubting other people's sincerity or questioning their intentions, your instincts are probably correct. You are less likely to regret being cautious than being too trusting.
> **Assignment:** Is it wise to be suspicious of the motives or honesty of other people, even those who appear to be trustworthy? Plan and write an essay in which you develop your point of view on this issue. Support your position with reasoning and examples taken from your reading, studies, experience, or observations. (SAT/College Board website)

This ACT prompt asks students to write about their perspective on a debatable issue:

> Educators debate extending high school to five years because of increasing demands on students from employers and colleges to participate in extracurricular activities and community service in addition to having high grades. Some educators support extending high school to five years because they think students need more time to achieve all that is expected of them. Other educators do not support extending high school to five years because they think students would lose interest in school and attendance would drop in the fifth year. In your opinion, should high school be extended to five years?
> **Assignment:** In your essay, take a position on this question. You may write about either one of the two points of view given, or you may present a different point of view on this question. Use specific reasons and examples to support your position. (ACT website)

The best way to prepare students for any specific test is to provide practice with prompts designed for the test they will be taking. You can find sample prompts and examples of scored essays for the ACT and SAT tests at www.act.org and www.sat.com.

TIPS FOR STUDENTS PREPARING TO WRITE AN ESSAY IN A TIMED TESTING SITUATION

1. Answer the Prompt

- First, it's important for students to understand the prompt since many tests automatically assign a score of 'o' for off-topic essays. Some prompts are oddly phrased so that students really think about what is being asked. If a prompt is unclear, students should try re-reading the excerpt and consider what question or issue the prompt is really asking them to address.

- A useful strategy is to turn the prompt into a rhetorical question and use it as the hook for the introduction. For example, an acceptable "hook" for the third prompt above might be: "Should schools extend high school to five years?" A rhetorical question will serve as the introduction, help students get started writing productively, and engrain the topic in their minds so they'll be less likely to stray off-topic.

- Students should avoid spending too much time on the introduction to this essay. A good introduction takes time to craft. For the purposes of a timed essay, a functional introduction is all students need: introduce the topic (a rhetorical re-framing of the prompt will do this), a brief comment about the topic—possibly observing the perplexity of the issue—and either a thesis statement that answers the prompt or a statement of the intention to discuss it in the body of the essay.

- Students must provide a clear answer to the prompt, whether in their introduction or conclusion. Since most tests require students to take a position, wishy-washy responses may score lower than unambiguous ones, even when students believe that both sides of an issue have merit.

2. Design the Essay Appropriately

- One approach to writing the paper is to treat it as a typical five-paragraph essay with a thesis statement at the end of the introduction—i.e., "In this essay, I will argue that schools should not extend high school to five years"—followed by three body paragraphs that support that position with reasoning, observations, and examples.

- A second strategy is to state an intention to explore the issue at the end of the introductory paragraph: "In this essay, I will discuss this issue." Students may choose this strategy when they honestly don't know how they want to answer the prompt. Then, they can write the first body paragraph in favor of the position and the second paragraph against it (or vice versa), providing strong supporting examples and reasoning for both positions. Then, for the third body paragraph, they must decide which position they find strongest and give it their best support. For this type of essay, students must make sure to answer the prompt clearly and unambiguously in the conclusion: "Thus, high school should *not* be extended."

3. Support Topic Sentences

- Paragraphs should begin with a topic sentence that makes an assertion about the essay topic. Most topic sentence assertions can be supported with examples or observations; students should close paragraphs with a sentence that reiterates the point. Students can think of this as an "Example Sandwich," in which the topic sentence and reiteration are the outside layers and the example, whether from observations, academic learning, or experience, form the "meat" of the sandwich.

Topic Sentence	Success leads to more difficulty in math, where mastering lessons leads to more difficult challenges.
Personal Observation	Young children learn to count first and then add. Next, they memorize multiplication tables. Eventually, they learn algebra, geometry, and calculus. In order to progress, students must face increasingly difficult challenges.
Reiteration	Therefore, success leads to more difficulty.

Topic Sentence	People adjust their behavior when faced with a threat.
3 Generic Observations	Children will eat their vegetables if dessert is on the line. Students will study for a test if faced with summer school. Drivers will respect the speed limit if a police car appears in the rear view mirror.
Reiteration	A threat motivates people to adjust the way they behave.

Topic Sentence	Truth does not depend on circumstances but on character.
Personal Experience	Once, I discovered an unpaid-for item in the bottom of my shopping cart after leaving a store. I didn't really have time to go back and pay for it, but I knew that if I didn't, I would have stolen that item. That I didn't mean to steal it wouldn't change the fact that I had, so I went back to pay.
Reiteration	While circumstances might permit me to make excuses, truth demands justice and integrity.

4. Incorporate Examples from Academic Subjects

- If at all possible, incorporate an example from literature, history, or another academic subject. An example from history often works best with prompts that ask students to ponder societal issues:

Topic Sentence	The media often influences people's values.
Example from History	When Upton Sinclair wrote *The Jungle*, people were outraged. Teddy Roosevelt read it and gave up sausage, even though he liked it. He instituted inspection laws to make sure food was safe to eat and production was not too cruel to workers.
Reiteration	Clearly, the media influences the way people think.

- Use an example from literature when the prompt concerns moral issues or ethics:

Topic Sentence	People adjust their behavior when faced with a threat.
Example from Literature	For example, in Margaret Mitchell's *Gone with the Wind*, when Scarlett O'Hara realizes that Melanie was her only true friend, she finally humbles herself to admit her love for Rhett Butler.
Reiteration	The threat of being completely alone compels Scarlet to change her behavior.

- When citing examples from literature, students should choose literary works that assessors will recognize and assume that whoever reads their essay will be familiar with the work from the author and title. Then, rather than summarizing the entire plot, students should focus on just the part of the work that supports their premise.

6. Finish Strong

- Normally, a conclusion reiterates a position and ends resonantly, but students shouldn't worry too much about the rhetorical strength of the conclusion in a timed essay. Assessors base scores more on how well students support positions in the body than on how conclusive they sound at the end.

- If students have time, they can make minor revisions by putting numbers in front of paragraphs to re-order them, drawing a line through any unnecessary words, off-topic sentences, or paragraphs that didn't pan out. They may also use a carrot symbol to insert missing words.

- Students should focus on what matters most: no one expects a timed essay to contain perfect handwriting, spelling, or word choices, but straying off-topic, contradicting themselves, or failing to support premises will be reflected in a low score. On the other hand, if an essay demonstrates good organization and strong support for a clear response, the overall score will not be affected by minor grammar or spelling errors.

- The last and best tip: practice! Students should try to write out at least three practice essays before the big day. Not only will they build up their handwriting stamina, they'll feel more confident and be able to focus better.

SAMPLE OPINIONATED POSITION ESSAY

The essay below will give you a sense of what a position essay looks like. For samples of essays that scored both high and low, visit www.act.com and www.sat.collegeboard.com.

On Telling Lies, White and Otherwise

Is it ever okay to tell a lie? At first, I'm tempted to say that lying is always wrong. But at the same time, I realize that the question is not that simple. People tell 'white lies' all the time — like when people ask how you are, and you have a sore throat. Even though you're not feeling great, you say 'fine,' thinking that it's not worth the trouble explaining why you're not. But what about other situations, situations where your answer matters more? When, if ever, is it right to tell a lie?

Most people would agree that in general you should tell the truth, even when it is tempting not to. People might be tempted to lie when they fear the reaction of another person, such as when you disobey your parents and you don't want to get punished. It might be convenient to tell a lie, but ultimately your parents might find out, and you might wind up deeper in trouble than you would have been in the first place. An even worse consequence, though, would be to avoid any punishment and conclude that telling lies is a good idea. You might decide to lie again, and before long, you will have become a dishonest person in general. Therefore, it is good to tell the truth in large part because to do otherwise is to compromise your integrity.

Of course, truthfulness is almost always best, but in some cases, lying may be necessary. For example, in *The Hiding Place*, Corrie ten Boom and her family harbored Jews in their home to prevent their deportation by the Nazis. Because the lives of several people depended on Corrie's ability to keep the Nazis from finding their hiding place, Corrie prepared herself to lie to the Nazis convincingly. When the Nazis did raid the house and demand to know the whereabouts of the Nazi refugees, Corrie insisted she knew of no Jews in the house. Although the Nazis arrested Corrie and her family, the Jews escaped. In this case, lying, if not ideal, was justifiable.

But situations like those are rare; most of the time, people lie to avoid punishment or to profit in some way. For instance, one time a guy came to our house to sell my parents a security system. He said that our neighborhood had been selected to try out the system for free. We didn't particularly want a security system, but since it was free, my mom said it would be okay. Then the salesman asked her to sign a piece of paper that said in tiny print that there would be a monthly charge of two hundred dollars. When my mom asked about it, the salesman said he never claimed that the service was free, just the system. Not mentioning the two hundred dollar monthly service charge was deceptive; clearly, the guy had forgotten to mention the fee because he wanted to make his commission on the sale.

Whereas an honest person seeks to be truthful at all times, a dishonest person cares more about the immediate consequences. If there's a personal advantage to lying, they see no reason not to. The honest person never lies unless consequences are dire and no other option remains. Therefore, I would say that telling lies might be justified in extreme situations, but these situations are so rare that qualification is almost unnecessary: for most people and in most situations, it's really not okay to lie.

Chapter 14

Applications & First Impressions

This chapter offers advice for those students who are applying for college or for their first jobs. Happily, any student who has completed the first half of this composition course should be more than capable of composing letters of introduction and application essays in order to successfully attain these purposes.

One piece of advice that will serve writers in any situation that calls for functional communication is to be selective with information. Many adolescent writers have a hard time discerning what information to include in application essays and cover letters and what to leave out, and the resulting essays and letters reflect this uncertainty. Sometimes, young writers hurt their own chances by including information that doesn't belong or by omitting information that would serve their ends. These students need to pause and reflect before trying to write. Students need to ask themselves what this person (or organization) is looking for in a candidate. I'm not suggesting that students falsify anything or merely curry favor; rather, students should first consider what the individual or organization they are addressing wants or needs to hear in order to make a decision about them and then consider how they can truthfully answer those concerns in their essay or letter.

APPLYING FOR COLLEGE ADMISSION

Some time ago, a young woman asked me to review the college application essay she'd written. In answer to a question included in the application materials, she'd explained why she wanted to attend this particular college: she wanted to be close to several friends who also planned to attend the school because of the area's excellent beaches. Now, this answer may have been honest, but such an answer could only have diminished her chances of actually getting into that particular college. Obviously, most future college students are going to anticipate a certain amount of recreation during their college years, but a college admissions officer wants to know that a prospective student wants to attend classes, benefit from a particular course of study, or participate in the college community. To answer a college application essay question with information about plans to have fun was completely off the mark.

The same goes for job applications. Many high school students write ineffective cover letters and resumes, either because they feel like none of their experiences are relevant or because they feel like all of their experiences are. The truth is somewhere in between: some of their experiences most likely will impress a prospective employer, and some won't. The trick is to highlight whatever ability the employer needs from the person in the position that is available. A student applying for a position as a restaurant server might want to highlight social skills and possibly some positive experiences as a team player; the same student applying for a position stocking goods would emphasize being a team player but probably not mention great social skills—a stocker who's always socializing is not going to be getting much work done.

Thus, students should tailor functional communication to suit each unique situation:

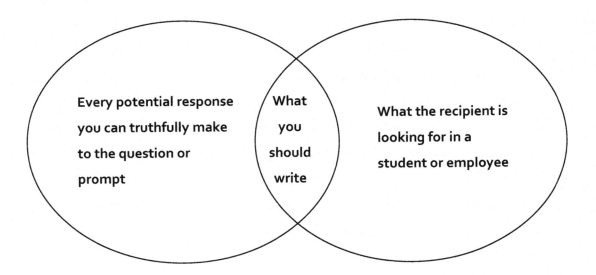

Every potential response you can truthfully make to the question or prompt

What you should write

What the recipient is looking for in a student or employee

What to Include in an Application Essay

College administrators consider the institutions they work for to be unique. Students who acknowledge that uniqueness write more effective responses in their college application essays. In their responses to posed questions, students should mention specific academic and extra-curricular programs, unique values or characteristics of the school, or aspects of the college's mission or vision that especially appeal to them. They should also investigate what qualities the college administrators are looking for in an applicant's essay.

Some schools have specific questions for students to answer, while others invite students to submit any essay that they have written in the course of their studies. For these, students should consider what the essay they choose to submit says about themselves: an academically correct, five-paragraph informative essay might prove to college administrators that they can compose an essay, but an argument about a topic of personal interest says more. Students do well to submit writing samples that clearly reflect their passionate interests or values, and if they haven't written such papers already, they would be wise to take the time to construct one rather than submit something that says little or nothing about themselves.

APPLYING FOR A JOB

Having worked in the personnel departments of two organizations, I know that many employers receive application materials from far more applicants than they can possibly hire, and all but a few of the applications simply get filed away. A few exceptional applications, however, don't. Managers often tuck the applications that impress them most into a special drawer, and when a position becomes available, they turn to those applications first to see if any of them fit the opening. Applicants who submit just the required application form rarely make this cut, but those who submit a carefully composed cover letter and resume, even if the business doesn't require one, much more frequently do.

Composing a Resume

The whole reason for putting together a resume is to impress a prospective employer enough to get a personal interview. That most employers get too many applications means that anyone who wants to impress a prospective employer has to appear motivated, qualified, and professional. A well-written resume and cover letter say all of that. Most employers don't have a lot of time to waste perusing applications for positions they don't need to fill. A properly composed resume and cover letter arrange information so that a prospective employer can quickly see whether an applicant has potential or not.

Many people feel daunted by the idea of writing a resume because they're not sure what to include in it. I'm not going to go into all of the details of resume writing here, as many online resources offer templates and sample resumes that students can examine. I will, however, point out that a resume should help a prospective employer quickly learn what kind of job an applicant wants and what kind of qualifications that applicant has. An employer wants to be able to glance at a resume and see a clear objective such as 'to work with animals' or 'to gain experience performing office work' and a list of qualifications, which will include both education and work experience. Work experience may be paid or unpaid; the important thing is the experience: what has a candidate actually *done*?

Students sometimes worry that they have nothing to include in the work experience section of a resume, especially if they've never held a paid position in the past. This, however, is not a problem because unpaid work experiences count—the important thing is to have experiences working, and most of the teenagers who are eager to work will find that they have plenty of experience to draw from if they have ever volunteered with an organization or even just helped someone out with a special chore on occasion.

Accurate verbs and parallel structures in the work experience section make for the most effective resumes. Lists of specific verbs conjugated in the past tense describe work experiences as accurately and concisely as possible. Even though the page may not be cluttered with words, employers can tell the difference between exaggerated attempts to impress them and accurate if limited descriptions. And accuracy is key: consider even the distinction between "Maintained lawn and garden" and "Did lawn work." The verb 'maintained' implies that the lawn was responsibly kept nice over a period of time, whereas 'did' merely suggests that lawn work was done, maybe just once. A potential employer may well notice the subtle difference.

A resume should also be neatly formatted, so that the job title, employer, location and general timeframe are listed in a consistent manner. There are many ways to do this, but here is one example:

Work Experience

Volunteer Shelver   2010 - present

    Local Public Library   Anytown, Michigan

    Shelved, stamped, organized, and sorted books.

Volunteer Food Server   2007 - present

    Hungry Soup Kitchen   Anytown, Michigan

    Prepared and served food once a month.

Caretaker   September 2011

    Jim and Sue Jamison   Anytown, Michigan

    Provided animal care by feeding, watering, and exercising owner's dogs. Maintained property by watering plants, retrieving mail, and shoveling driveway.

Many times, informal work experiences involve no formal title, but students may invent one so long as the title they make up reflects the work done. Also, it's appropriate to precede the title with the word 'Volunteer' if no compensation was involved. Finally, if a position involved more than five specific activities, consider grouping the activities by their larger function. Retain the parallel structure by conjugating the larger function with a past tense verb and listing the subsidiary activities afterwards as gerunds (i.e., by *watering* plants, *retrieving* mail, etc.) as in the third experience example above.

Notice that the activities are described in the past tense and with little elaboration. A resume need not clarify how well a task was performed; the resume merely shows potential employers what the applicant has done—that is, what qualifications the applicant has. A resume should not attempt to convince an employer of the probable quality of the applicant's performance. Not only can the employer not trust an applicant's assessment of his or her own quality of performance, reading an applicant's unhelpful self-appraisal only wastes the employer's time, which of course no one appreciates. A resume that lists qualifications clearly and simply impresses employers, who then will decide whether or not an applicant seems to be a good fit for a position during a personal interview.

Writing Cover Letters

Many people also feel uncertain about writing cover letters. As with resumes, they often feel the need to praise themselves and flatter a prospective employer. Unfortunately, that misunderstanding sometimes leads students to write groveling cover letters like this:

Dear Hiring Manager;

I enjoy doing good work and your company has an admirable reputation.

Being a hard worker, I may indirectly save money and time for your company. I can bring cooperation and a good attitude to the job. Even though I am young and have not held a lot of jobs, my enthusiasm and reliability will be a productive asset to your company. One can reach me at 345-123-4567. I am ready to do my best to be a desired addition to your excellent company if you hire me for this position.

Thank you so much for your consideration.

Sincerely,

Joe Simpson

Although this person clearly has an idea about what a cover letter should accomplish, just about everything in it is slightly off because it includes information that should be excluded and omits information that should be included. In short, it contains the wrong information.

A cover letter should provide an introduction for the applicant and the applicant's enclosed resume and suggest reasons why the applicant might appeal to the potential employer as an employee. If there is some particular reason why an applicant wants to work for a particular employer at a particular time, this explanation might follow, but if the applicant just wants a job and doesn't have a preference for one employer over another, it's best not to engage in empty flattery. Thus a cover letter should answer the questions a prospective employer is likely to have in the order he or she is like to have them:

- Who are you and what do you want from me?
- Why should I be interested in you?
- Seeing as you have all those great qualities, why do you need a job?
- Why do you want this job as opposed to another?
- How can I contact you?

Dear Hiring Manager;

I am writing to submit my resume for consideration in your search for a Coffeehouse Barista. As you will see from my resume, I have extensive experience as a volunteer food server for local charities. Most recently, I spent a summer working as a volunteer staff member at Wholesome Summer Camp, where I learned to comply with orders, work with a team, and respond quickly and cheerfully to minor emergencies of all kinds.

As a high school senior with college in my near future, I am eager to get a job and start saving money for tuition. I have frequented your coffeehouse in the past and enjoy the pleasant atmosphere; also, the proximity of your establishment to my home would make it easy for me to bike to work. In addition, as a home school student, I can be very flexible in terms of scheduling. If you have any questions, please contact me at 345–123-4567. Thank you for your consideration.

Sincerely,

Michelle Saunders

Communicating for Functional Purposes

Whether a student is applying for college or for a job, writing a business letter, logging a complaint, or even querying a publication in order to get a piece of writing published, when writing for a functional purpose, awareness of audience is key. The best instruction for students composing any kind of functional communication is to imagine what the recipient will be thinking at each stage: upon opening the letter, any recipient is going to wonder, "Who is writing to me, and what does this person want?" Or, upon receiving a college application, an admissions officer is going to ask, "What is this applicant going to bring to our school?" Whenever a student stalls and wonders what to write next, they need to ask, "What questions have I left hanging? What will my audience want to know now?"

Finally, remind students that all readers are lazy: they don't want to read three pages to find out what could have been said in one. Functional communication should always get to the point and rarely embellish. People in the real world may choose to read clever or creative writing in their leisure, but for the most part, they don't want to see semi-entertaining fluff at work. Think about it: everything in a piece of functional writing communicates something about the author. A student who puts irrelevant information and cracks jokes in a job application will be considered a little foolish, and he or she probably won't get the job. The applicant who anticipates a prospective employer's every question will seem unusually competent and effective. Chances are, if there's a job to be had, he or she will get it.

Chapter 15

Publication and Reflection

The basic and advanced level compositions outlined in this book are academic in purpose, audience, and tone. Certainly, their purposes—that is, to learn and to demonstrate learning—are academic, as are their audiences, who are, of course, teachers. Tone is a little more subtle, but basically an academic tone conveys as little as possible about a writer's attitude and as much as possible about the topic itself, usually in a neutral, third person voice, which means no I's, we's, or you's, especially in the body paragraphs. Of course, there is some room for deviation, especially with essays that reflect a student's perspective on an issue—and a few of the sample essays in Appendix D do deviate a bit—but by and large, academic essays stick to a pretty neutral tone most of the time. This is quite different from what you'd expect in a personal essay, which is where a writer expresses personal opinions and attitudes about a topic, often with ample commentary, snide remarks, and even sarcastic observations. Although such writings are often quite funny—Dave Barry is a genius in his own way—they're really not academic, nor do writers like Dave Barry pretend to be.

Most curriculums are designed to teach students to write for "a variety of purposes" and with "voice," and I disagree with those designs. As I have already argued, I don't believe people need to be able to write for expressive or imaginative purposes at all, and those who choose to do so usually have more success when they have learned to write clearly and coherently first. But what really confuses students these days is the emphasis on writing with "voice," which is a nebulous writing quality that I believe confuses high school students—sometimes so much that they cannot formulate a coherent essay at all.

What do educators mean by 'voice?' The State of Alaska's Student Assessment Rubric describes it as "highly individual" language with an interesting, flavorful tone, in which the "reader senses the person behind the words." Writers who lack voice seem "uncomfortable with the topic" and "unaware of [the] reader" (State of Alaska). English teacher Kelly Gallagher (2006) offers the following as an example of a writer with "strong voice:"

"That'll be ten dollars," you hear the cashier demand. Ten dollars! Can you believe it? Ten dollars to see a movie that is not really original. Ten dollars to see some hour-and-a-half-knock-off-wannabe-remake. "Digitally remastered!" my rear end . . . All these waste-of-time remakes are exactly the same characters and plotlines as they were twenty years ago. The only new things about them are the one-hit-wonder actors doing what they call "acting" in front of cheesy green screens. Whatever happened to the classics? Keyword here: classics. (p. 71)

This excerpt meets the criteria for "voice," but it falls short when it comes to clarity and coherence: I can't quite tell what the author's purpose or main point is—is the writer angry about the price of movie tickets or arguing for better quality movies—or some kind of return to the classics? It's hard to tell, because "voice" overpowers substance so that the piece is little more than an incoherent rant, full of invented spelling, sentence fragments, and logical gaps. Yes, the author's attitude comes across loud and clear, but is that what high school students need to learn—how to convey more attitude, less clearly? In most situations, I would have to say no: people who want to be taken seriously by serious people in the real world must be able to curtail their emotions and write coherently.

I believe this call for "voice" in student essays actually contradicts many of the principles of good writing students should be prioritizing and reflects a trend in Language Arts that previous writing teachers would have discouraged. William Strunk and E.B. White (1977) advised their students to "write in a way that draws the reader's attention to the sense and substance of the writing, rather than to the mood and temper of the author" (p. 70). They go on to suggest, "To achieve style, begin by affecting none" (p. 70). Contrast that advice with the student sample above and you will understand why I discourage teaching high school students to write with "voice" and focus instead on teaching them to clarify their thoughts and communicate them as eloquently and coherently as they can.

That being said, students who have developed the essential skills all writers need and who are eager to try something new should have the opportunity to experiment with writing for wider audiences. Of course, many of the students who are eager to try something new will be the ones who have voluntarily and independently been writing for non-academic purposes on their own—writing poetry and stories, personal essays, song lyrics, journal entries and the like. The key with challenging students to play around with voice and tone is to be clear about what writing is academic in purpose and what writing is not.

Recycling Papers

A great way to allow students who wish to learn how different audiences and purposes call for different tones and strategies is to revamp one of their previously written academic papers. For instance, students could turn a research paper into either an informative essay or a how-to article for a wider audience. An argument can easily become a persuasive article or an op-ed (opinionated essay) for a magazine or newspaper. Topics that are personally important to students can become reflections or personal essays. Any of these could be broken into smaller units and turned into a series for a blog. Each of these forms involves a slightly different purpose and audience, and students who are eager to try something new will appreciate the challenge of adjusting their already-formulated ideas on their topic to fit the bill. Rather than confusing students about tone, by converting writing they know is academic, students reinforce what constitutes a neutral tone and what constitutes styles and tones that are appropriate for other contexts.

How do you teach these other tones and purposes? You don't. Students who master advanced academic writing with clarity, coherence, eloquence, and correctness have developed the critical thinking ability to figure out what kind of writing they want to attempt and have seen in the writing of authors they'd like to imitate. This is exactly how many gifted writers learn: "the young poet generally begins his self-education by reading other poets and by imitating their voices as best he can" (Gardner, 2004, p. 82). William Zinsser says, "I learned [to write] by reading the men and women who were doing the kind of writing I wanted to do and trying to figure out how they did it" (2001, p. 35). So adolescent writers learn: by imitating the writing styles of authors they admire most.

Another reason to recycle papers is that students can take advantage of the research they've already done, permitting them to focus on researching writing techniques and styles. To learn how to write effectively for a wider audience, students should analyze what techniques work best for other writers of similar types of writing. For instance, a student who composed a research paper on the effects various energy sources have on the environment might want to write an article persuading an audience of the best solutions. Before starting to write an article, such a student should collect five or six articles that attempt to persuade people about solutions for complicated problems and identify what strategies were most and least effective in hooking readers in the introduction, holding readers and appeasing any dissenters in the body, and convincing them at the end.

Or say the student wanted to flip an argument around and give it a humorous spin. That student should gather a few humorous essays on semi-serious topics and see how effective humorists draw an audience in and hold them without the article seeming to peter out by the end. Humor, incidentally, is actually pretty tricky to do well. Adolescents are often drawn to it because it's obviously fun to engage in, but once you define a piece as humorous, a writer has to somehow surprise readers who have already been tipped off that hilarity is in store. That's actually a really hard expectation to live up to.

Writing for a Broader Audience

Although the best instruction for students who really want to achieve a particular purpose with their writing will come from their analysis of other authors, as before, I'm going to suggest a few issues that novice writers often confront when attempting to write for a general audience as opposed to an academic one.

First is **concision**. The guidelines for most newspapers, magazines and e-zines involve specific word count requirements. A research paper can easily run to 5,000 words or more, but a typical how-to article might need to be 1,500 or less. Obviously, a research paper must be more comprehensive than a how-to article, and the purposes are distinct, so a student will probably be able to get the word count down to maybe 3,000 or so just by adjusting the paper's purpose. Most students, however, hit a wall of sorts where they feel like they simply can't cut another word and retain their meaning. Almost always, however, they're wrong.

How do students reduce their word counts? Writing with precise subjects and active verbs goes a long way toward eliminating unnecessary words. When each word is at a premium, however, this precision becomes even more important. Zinsser (2001) puts it well:

> Verbs are the most important of all your tools . . . try to avoid the kind that need an appended preposition to complete their work. Don't set up a business that you can start or launch. Don't say that the president of the company stepped down. Did he resign? Did he retire? Did he get fired? Be precise. Use precise verbs. (p. 69)

Precise verbs will eliminate the need to subordinate important words in prepositional phrases and often the need to include adverbs as well. Choosing precise subjects and direct objects often reduces the need for descriptive adjectives as well.

Many teachers instruct students to spruce up their writing with descriptive adjectives and adverbs, when in fact, this is the worst possible advice for most writers, with the possible exception of humorists. Serious writers add adverbs and adjectives only when they are necessary to make sentences true. Adverbs I find essential generally clarify my precise meaning: "often," or "rarely," "always," "never," "not." The same is true for adjectives:

"some" or "many" helps me avoid unfairly characterizing people who don't all fit the same molds; "few" or "most," helps me clarify how widespread an issue may be without overstating my case.

Parallel sentence structures also tighten word counts, as do bullet lists. Students who use bullet lists should make sure that their lists are parallel in structure.

Secondly, **hooking an audience** really does matter when writing for a real audience. I am not going to try to give any instruction on this item except to point students to the non-fiction writers whose essays and articles they enjoy reading. Have them make a list of opening strategies they really admire, and suggest they keep a tally of the techniques they find most appealing. While they're at it, have them compare effective conclusions. The concluding line in any piece of writing should match the feeling the writer wants his or her audience to have upon finishing the piece.

The final issue with non-academic writing is **correctness**. Most students who read a lot will probably have already spotted this one: real writers—that is, people who write for non-academic audiences—break the rules. Constantly. Professional writers do all sorts of things that up to now have been more or less *verboten*. They compose paragraphs of one sentence and sentences of one word. They splice sentences and split infinitives. They start sentences with 'and' and end them with prepositions. You name it, real writers do it. And they get away with it.

One writer's adage says that you have to know the rules to know when you can break them. Once students have a solid background and sufficient practice with writing correctly, writing naturally comes easily. Incorrectness no longer distracts readers, it enhances prose. When students don't know what they're doing, errors make their ideas confusing. Their ideas don't come across in their writing, and they themselves seem uneducated and ineffective as communicators. That is why the essential course insisted on clarity first. When students understand how to get their ideas across clearly, they gradually get a feeling for how to communicate clearly, even when the grammar is not 100% technically correct.

Not every student gets to this point. Not every student wants to. That's okay—in fact, it's more than okay. We are all of us created as uniquely gifted individuals, and it's a wonderful thing that some of us love to write, but as someone who does, I think it's an even more wonderful thing some people are designed to love other things. I thank God for the people who love to care for sick patients or defend innocent people from harm or produce useful goods like the food and clothes we all need. As much as I love vivid words and well-crafted ideas, I'm glad most people aren't called to be writers.

Writing for a Real Audience Rubric

Criteria	Requires Revision	Acceptable	Excellent
Content: Introduction	The introduction has no "hook", provides no context/topic for the piece, or includes a formal, academic-style thesis statement	Begins with a mildly interesting "hook", provides a context/topic for the essay, and implies but does not reveal the thesis	Engages reader with a story or item of general interest, provides a context/topic for the essay, and suggests where the piece is going without revealing what it's going to say
Clarity: Subjects and Verbs; Sentence correctness	The writer prefers to convey ideas through adjectives and adverbs; verbs are nondescript and subjects vague; spelling or conventions errors distract the reader	The writer prefers the use of precise and active verbs and clear subjects; the essay contains less than two conventions errors per page	The writer prefers the use of precise and active verbs and clear subjects; any fragments are clearly intended for rhetorical effect
Coherence: Thoroughness and Order of Support	Sentences do not reflect any logical order; appear to be out-of-order or off-topic, and/or include logical gaps or redundancies	Sentences reflect a logical order and initiate with previously introduced ideas and establish new ideas; any gap or overlap of ideas is slight	Sentences occur in a logical order and establish new ideas, interrupting this progression only to clarify or qualify points; parenthetical comments entertain the reader
Eloquence: Sentence length, type, and endings	Sentences include grammatically awkward structures, repeat sentence patterns or fail to vary in length or type; concluding words lack emphasis or significance	Sentence length is mostly long; sentences do not repeat the same patterns; concluding statements emphasize final words	Sentences vary in length and structure; parallel structures are well-balanced (or potentially unbalanced for comic effect); a few pithy statements are intriguing or powerful
Eloquence: Tone	The piece is wordy and lacks precision, contains clichés, or uses literary devices ineffectively; a humorous approach to serious points gives the piece an air of inappropriateness	Words are apt and precise; one or more literary devices is used effectively	Words are apt and precise; one or more metaphors make powerful connections; the piece incorporates humor appropriately
Eloquence: Conclusion recalls previously introduced imagery or themes	The conclusion leaves the issue hanging or trails off ineffectively	The conclusion resolves the topic effectively but may fail to affect the reader emotionally	The conclusion effectively reiterates, resolves, or completes the introductory idea and leaves the reader with a specific feeling (i.e., resolved, amused, concerned, inspired)

Writing to Reflect

The last writing task I would like to describe here is the personal philosophy paper, which involves synthesizing opinionated ideas related to philosophical topics rather than factual ones. This assignment challenges students not only to state their opinions on some of life's deepest questions, but also to critically examine and reflect upon them.

Examining one's own opinions about issues such as politics and religion is not usually encouraged in public schools, but the exercise is extremely valuable, especially for people who live in a democracy. As Tocqueville noticed over two hundred years ago, most democratic people tend to habitually adopt popular opinions as their own without ever critically considering them (p. 179). In a country that has become as polarized in terms of political, moral, and spiritual beliefs as ours, this is a dangerous tendency.

It is a core value for Americans that all people have the right to hold and express opinions about all kinds of philosophical matters, but most people don't realize that this freedom of speech and thought actually comes at a price. Because anyone in a democracy can circulate opinions, we are all bombarded, daily, by the opinions of others, many of which are incompatible with our own. Because people feel uncomfortable suspending judgment yet lack the time or energy to critically examine so many opinions, most learn the "habit of believing firmly without reflecting" (Tocqueville, p. 179). In fact, many people regularly reform their opinions to conform to the views most popular among the company they keep.

When young people leave home to attend college, students who have not learned to examine their convictions easily fall prey to opinionated professors who consider it their duty to convince students that whatever their parents believed should be discarded, arguing that parents have a sort of unfair sway, something akin to brainwashing, that makes students' convictions inauthentic and thus automatically wrong (because of their supposed inauthenticity). Stripped of their support system, psychologically vulnerable college students tend to adopt the beliefs of the most charismatic professor they encounter, even if that belief system ultimately contradicts what they had previously considered to be true. Students who read and write about and critically examine their own beliefs will not be so easily swayed to abandon them simply because someone "older and wiser" is passionate about his.

Knowing that Kristen's beliefs would be challenged in every way when she left home, the last assignment I gave her as a high school senior was to synthesize her personal philosophy with the prompt, "What do you believe and why?" Because I knew this would be my last opportunity to influence her, I gave her a pile of readings from authors like C.S.

Lewis, Thomas a Kempis, Dietrich Bonhoeffer, Walter Brueggemann, and N.T. Wright to help her think through her ideas. Admittedly, I still wanted to influence her, but I also made it clear that I wanted her to write this paper to reflect her personal convictions and not merely to please me.

I have to say, no matter what anyone says, a parent only has so much sway over their child's attitudes, beliefs, and behaviors. Although that may be especially true of teenagers and young adults, I remember observing, when I was expecting Kristen, how I could not control her movements: she would not kick on command for her father's benefit nor would she stop kicking for mine.

So it was with Kristen's personal philosophy paper. In spite of the many resources I'd given her to read, in the end, my daughter embraced just a few of them and said, "Eh," to the rest. She organized her paper around the worship songs and hymns she loved best, and chose the Bible as the authoritative source backing most of her assertions. And in response to my concern that she had only inherited her father's and my faith, she wrote (much to my surprise) that she had only recently discovered God's power in her life, when she emerged unscathed from a car accident which had demolished the passenger side of her friend's car:

> Sitting in the ruined car with glass in my hair and many people talking loudly and anxiously all around me, I could not wrap my mind around what had just happened. I didn't even realize at first how bad it had been. When I got out of the car – I had to crawl out the driver's side, since the passenger door wouldn't open – I realized that the other truck had hit the car just inches away from where I'd been, and that the car was dented inwards by several feet. I couldn't believe I'd escaped with nothing more than bruises. That's when I envisioned the hand of God protecting me from harm . . . That's when it clicked in my mind that this faith stuff was real. (K. Luchsinger, personal communication, April 4, 2011)

Kristen's personal philosophy paper would never have been required of her in a public school, probably because most teachers would find it difficult to objectively grade papers reflecting widely divergent religious and political views. As teaching parents, however, assigning such a paper can be deeply satisfying. No, Kristen did not relish the same excerpts I did, nor did she express her faith as I would have, but what she did relish and write was meaningful to her, and no matter what anyone tells her as she moves on, she knows that what she believes has not been merely force-fed to her from birth. Though the essay was assigned, Kristen knows that what she wrote was authentic.

References

Adler, M. & Van Doren, C. (1972). *How to read a book: The classic guide to intelligent reading.* New York: Simon & Schuster.

Arnow, H. (1954). *The dollmaker.* New York: Avon Books.

Berger, P., Berger, B., and Kellner, H. (1973). *The homeless mind: Modernization and consciousness.* New York: Vintage Books.

Bromley, K., Irwin DeVitis, L., & Modlo, M. (1999). *50 graphic organizers for reading, writing & more: Reproducible templates, student samples, and easy strategies to support every learner.* USA: Scholastic Professional.

Christenbury, L., Gere, A., & Sassi, K. (2005). *Writing on demand: Best practices and strategies for success.* Portsmouth, NH: Heinemann.

Conspiracy Theory. (n.d.) Retrieved from http://en.wikipedia.org/wiki/Conspiracy_theory

Dewey, J. (1938). *Experience and education.* New York: Simon & Schuster.

Gallagher, K. (2006). *Teaching adolescent writers.* Portland, ME: Stenhouse.

Hacker, D. (2004). *Rules for writers.* United States: Bedford/St. Martin's.

Gardner, H. (2004). *Frames of mind: The theory of multiple intelligences.* New York: Basic Books.

Goertzel, T. (1994). Belief in Conspiracy Theories. *Political Psychology, 15* Retrieved from http://crab.rutgers.edu/~goertzel/CONSPIRE.docSimilar

Grandin, T., and Johnson, C. (2005). *Animals in translation: Using the mysteries of autism to decode animal behavior.* Orlando, FL: Harcourt.

Haddon, M. (2003). *The curious incident of the dog in the night-time.* USA: Random House.

Harding, N. (2011, Nov. 12). Truth and lies: Conspiracy theories are running rampant thanks to modern technology. *The Independent.* http://www.independent.co.uk/

Harvey, M. (2003). *The nuts and bolts of college writing.* USA: Hackett.

Johnson, G. (1998). *Biology: Visualizing life.* FL: Holt, Rinehart and Winston.

Kenrick, D. (2011, July 15). Why the human brain is designed to distrust. *Psychology Today.* Retrieved from http://www.psychologytoday.com/

Lutz, W. (1989). *Doublespeak.* New York: Harper Collins.

McGuinness, D. (1997). *Why our children can't read and what we can do about it: A scientific revolution in reading.* New York: Touchstone.

Nasar, S. (1998). *A beautiful mind.* New York: Touchstone.

Noden, H. (1999). *Using grammatical structures to teach writing.* Portsmouth, NH: Boynton/Cook Heinemann.

O'Neill, D. (1994). *The firecracker boys: H-Bombs, Inupiat eskimos, and the roots of the environmental movement.* Philadelphia, PA: Basic Books.

Ragone, N. (2004). *The everything American government book.* Avon, MA: Adams Media.

Rand, A. (2001). *The art of nonfiction: A guide for writers and readers.* USA: Penguin.

Rutter, D. (2003, May). Gleanings: A growing concern: Hazardous waste in fertilizer. *The New Farm.* Retrieved from http://rodaleinstitute.org/

Shaffer, M. (2001). Waste lands: The threat of toxic fertilizer. Retrieved from California Public Interest Research Group website http://www.pirg.org/toxics/reports/wastelands/WasteLands.pdf

Shermer, M. (2009, Sept. 10). Why people believe in conspiracies. *Scientific American.* Retrieved from http://www.scientificamerican.com/sciammag/

Snyder, C. (2011, June). Biosolids are not a fertilizer. *Farming Magazine.* Retrieved from http://www.farmingmagazine.com/default.aspx

State of Alaska Department of Education. (n.d.) Alaska comprehensive system of student assessment: 6-point holistic rubric for scoring the extended-constructed response essay on the writing subtests of the High School Graduation Qualifying Examination. Retrieved from http://www.eed.state.ak.us/tls/assessment/HSGQE/CTB6PointWritingRubric.pdf

State University of New Jersey, Rutgers. (2006). Public health concerns with hazardous materials in fertilizers. *The Soil Profile.* Retrieved from http://njaes.rutgers.edu/pubs/soilprofile/sp-v16.pdf

Storing, H. (Ed.). (1981). *The complete anti-federalist.* Chicago: University of Chicago Press, Retrieved from http://press-pubs.uchicago.edu/founders/documents/v1ch8s26.html

Strunk, W. & White, E. (1979). *The elements of style.* New York: MacMillan.

Essay Type	Comparison or Contrast Essay
Academic Prompt	Compare similarities between two distinct occupations.
Answer 1	Both mechanics and doctors diagnose problems
Answer 2	Both mechanics and doctors prescribe remedies
Answer 3	Both car mechanics and doctors perform operations to fix problems
Thesis Statement	Although mechanics and doctors are rarely considered similar professions, both diagnose problems, prescribe remedies, and perform operations.

Topic Sentence

Use the three answers you already generated as paragraph topics. Begin body paragraphs with a topic sentence, which tells readers what the paragraph will be about. One way to write a topic sentence is by connecting the essay topic to the paragraph topic. For example, in an essay about healthy habits, one of the paragraphs might be about exercise. A topic sentence for this paragraph might be:

One healthy habit that people should practice is physical exercise.

Include a transition in topic sentences for the second and third body paragraphs.

Another healthy habit involves eating a balanced diet.

Finally, a healthy person should avoid falling out of airplanes.

As you get used to writing topic sentences, you will probably see that you don't actually need to literally write the essay topic in the sentence so much as make an assertion that is logically tied to the essay topic. That's okay—in fact, it's really good. Subtle topic sentences define the scope of a paragraph as well as the more obvious ones above. In fact, I would say that you should use the clunkier kind only as long as you're still trying to figure out what to write for a topic sentence. Once topic sentences make sense to you, just write the assertion that comes next in your progression.

You might wonder if you need a topic sentence for every body paragraph. For now, the answer is yes. Eventually, you may get to a point where your paragraphs are so long that you need to break them up just so that they don't look boring to readers. Then, you won't have a topic sentence for every paragraph. For now, however, topic sentences help readers follow you and help you stay on task. Those are good things.

Explanations, Examples, and Extras, Oh My!

Follow your topic sentence with a sentence that responds to what the reader needs to know next. In most essays, the reader will want to know one of three things:

- Why do you say that?
- Can you give me an example of that?
- What do you mean by that?

In other words, a topic sentence will normally be followed by

- A sentence that explains or clarifies your last sentence
- An example that proves your last assertion
- A sentence that adds more detail to the last idea described

Most of the remaining 3 – 9 sentences in the paragraph will answer one of those three questions about the last idea conveyed in the previous sentence. If you get stuck, ask each question about the last sentence you wrote and consider whether it is what readers would ask as well. If so, answering that question is the next task in developing the paragraph.

Typical Patterns of Development

Many types of paragraphs develop with fairly predictable patterns. Originally, I was going to include blank templates for some of these, but ultimately I opted to leave them out. Not only can you jot 'topic sentence,' 'clarification,' 'example,' and so on in the margins of your own paper, the truth is that the patterns that often work don't always work. The more I tutor, the more I realize that there are no magic patterns: how a paragraph develops really depends on you and the ideas you want to express.

That being said, the next pages suggest a few patterns to help you if you get stuck. There is a logic to what comes next in a given paragraph and really a very limited number of ways to proceed. The template on page 211 lists these. If you're having a hard time writing paragraphs, try using the template and, with each sentence, consider which type of sentence needs to come next. A few of the options will always be easy to eliminate, and a few of the options will often seem pretty feasible. Shoot for feasible and whatever you write will probably be right on.

Wrap-Up (Although actually this one's optional)

Include a wrap-up sentence if the paragraph seems to need one or if the paragraph is on the short side. The wrap-up sentence should connect the last idea discussed back to the paragraph topic.

How to Develop a Body Paragraph in a Classification Essay

Since many topic sentences broadly announce the topic of the paragraph, most progressions need a sentence to clarify more precisely what the topic sentence meant. After this clarification, readers look for an example that supports the point being made as well as a sentence or two that provides additional details about the example that, once again, agree with the point being made in the paragraph. Depending on how well the first example supports the topic sentence, another example and details about it may follow. A wrap-up sentence, while optional, makes the paragraph feel complete.

Topic Sentence	A few of the characters in *The Lord of the Rings* are always good.
Clarification	Usually, these characters stand for purity in some way.
Example	The elves, for instance, serve as stewards of their world who are never deceived or tempted by the desire to rule.
Detail	When they appear in the first book, their singing wards off the Black Riders, who are seeking Frodo in order to capture the One Ring, and the elves harbor Frodo and offer him advice. Although Sauron used the rings he made to corrupt the dwarves and men, the elves were so good and pure that Sauron was never able to corrupt them for his purposes.
Example	Another example of a purely good character is Tom Bombadil.
Detail	Like the elves, Frodo's ring has no power over him because he has no desire to rule. Because Tom Bombadil is content, he is a wise steward in his realm that even the willow trees willingly obey, but because he does not demand control, he never seems like a tyrant.
Wrap-up (Optional)	Both the elves and Bombadil feel humility before creation, and so both use their powers for preservation of all that is good.

How to Develop a Body Paragraph in an Exemplification Essay

Some paragraphs develop by providing illustrative examples in support of a topic sentence. In these paragraphs a topic sentence will make a generalization or a vague statement about a topic which will then be followed by one lengthy example or sometimes two or three short examples of whatever the generalization is about. These paragraphs may allow for a few brief details, but the main support for the topic sentences come through illustrations, which describe exactly what led the writer to make the topic sentence generalization. A wrap-up sentence, while optional, makes the paragraph feel complete.

Topic Sentence	Owl, who others consider to be highly educated, is condescending.
Example	He tells Rabbit to go away because he is busy thinking,
Detail	as if his thinking were so important that it should not be interrupted.
Example	Later, he feels irritated when Rabbit asks Owl about Christopher Robin's note and doesn't acknowledge that he can't read it. Instead, he waits until Rabbit gives him enough information to hazard an impressive-sounding guess as to its meaning.
Detail	Even though Rabbit is actually more knowledgeable than Owl, Owl never lets on that he's even more clueless than Rabbit.
Wrap-up (Optional)	Owl's condescending attitude intimidates most of the other animals in the Hundred Acre Wood, and although they admire and accept him in their group, Owl has no close friends as a result.

How to Develop a Body Paragraph in a Process Essay

A good strategy for a paragraph in a concrete process essay is to simply describe steps in the process, adding details as needed. A wrap-up sentence makes the paragraph feel complete.

Topic Sentence	The next day, we bake the cookies.
1st Step 2nd Step Detail Detail 3rd Step Detail 4th Step 5th Step 6th Step Detail 7th Step	We preheat the oven before doing anything else. Then, we prepare the dough. After removing it from the plastic wrap, we divide the dough into three parts and store two in the refrigerator until we need them. Then we sprinkle flour on the work surface and roll the dough to about ¼ inch thickness with a rolling pin. Making sure to dip the cookie cutters in flour, we choose our favorite shapes and press them into the dough. We carefully place the shapes on a cookie sheet. Once we have filled the sheet, we put in the pre-heated oven and bake the cookies until just a touch of golden brown appears around the edges of the cookies. At that point, we remove them from the oven and transfer them to a cooling rack.
Wrap-up	When the cookies cool, we store them in plastic containers.

How to Develop a Body Paragraph in an Explanatory Essay

Follow the topic sentence in an explanatory essay with a sentence that clarifies the topic sentence. In the example below, the second sentence "What do you mean by 'wasting kids' time'?" The next two sentences give details that explain and support the second sentence, while the wrap-up sentence connects the last idea discussed (waiting on a teacher) back to the essay topic (homeschool).

Topic Sentence	Many families decide to homeschool because public schools waste kids' time.
Explain Topic Sentence	In public schools, a lot of activities have more to do with the teacher's need to organize a classroom of students than with the students' need to learn.
Detail	Teachers spend a lot of time explaining rules, getting kids to behave, and telling students to get books out, put things away, quiet down, or line up.
Detail	During lessons, students spend a lot of time waiting to be called on to ask or answer questions, waiting for classmates to catch up, and waiting for teachers to deal with kids who aren't paying attention or who are causing problems.
Wrap-up	Even though homeschool students sometimes have to wait while their parents help siblings or do chores, a lot less time is wasted in a homeschool setting.

How to Develop a Body Paragraph in a Persuasive Essay

A persuasive essay develops much like an explanatory essay: you need to provide good reasons and reasonable support for whatever you suggest should happen. Therefore, the paragraph develops with clarification of the writer's ideas and the writer's reasoning about the topic.

Topic Sentence	Replacing phone books with new ones every year wastes resources.
Explain Topic Sentence	An estimated five million tress are cut down each year to print the white pages alone, and only about a quarter of the people who get phone books recycle them.
Reasoning	Even if some of the phone companies opt to use recycled paper when they print new books, they're still using a lot of ink and gas to transport the books.
Reasoning	People who recycle unwanted phone books are still wasting resources because it takes more gas to carry them to the recycling center.
Wrap-up	That's a lot of waste, especially when you multiply the number of households receiving phone books by two or three.

How to Develop a Body Paragraph in a Comparison and Contrast Essay

A comparison and contrast paragraph develops much like an explanatory essay, with the topic sentence identifying either a similarity or distinction between two concepts and the second sentence clarifying the first. This point is then supported with examples and details that either compare or contrast the two items, maintaining the same order of discussion for each. Of all of the paragraphs described here, this is the one you're most likely to need to outline in order to keep your organization straight.

Topic Sentence	Another example of two fruits that sound similar but seem different are the naranja and the naranjilla.
Clarification Sentence	In Spanish, 'naranja' means 'orange.'
1st Example	As in English, a 'naranja' is an orange, which is round and orange, both inside and outside.
Detail	The rind of an orange may be thick or thin, and the flesh sometimes varies from pale to bright orange, depending on the variety.
Detail	Although some varieties of oranges are firm and good for eating, many oranges are so juicy that they are squeezed and turned into orange juice that people can drink unsweetened.
2nd Example	In contrast, the naranjilla is a smaller fruit that is mainly orange but usually with swirls of deep green.
Detail	The naranjilla's rind is thin, which is why the fruit bruises easily, but the juicy flesh of the fruit is as brightly green as fresh basil leaves.
Detail	The flavor of the fruit, however, is so tart as to be nearly inedible. Diluted with water and sweetened with sugar, however, naranjillas make a frothy green juice that is extraordinarily delicious.
Wrap-up	Naranjillas and oranges, while outwardly similar, taste very different.

The final section of this book provides several sample five-paragraph essays. I include these so that you and your student can get a feel for what the various types of essays look like as well as what range of topics and tones are acceptable in a five-paragraph essay. These essays can serve as teaching tools if you like. You can ask students to analyze these essays by asking any of the questions below.

Questions for Analysis

- What is the essay topic? How do you know?

- Is the topic familiar to the writer, something he or she just wanted to write about, or do you think this essay was assigned for a specific academic class?

- Does this essay contain a thesis statement or an announcement of intent?

- Do topic sentences obviously connect essay and paragraph topics, or are they more subtle? How do subtle topic sentences relate to the essay topic?

- What is the primary logical order of the paragraphs? (Logical orders are chronological, causal, analogical, and topical.) Is there secondary order?

- Do the paragraphs occur in the best possible order?

- Do the supporting examples and details explain or expand each topic sentence?

- Can you distinguish examples from details?

- What transitions are used? In your opinion, are more transitions needed?

- Does the tone in the introduction and conclusion paragraphs differ from that of body paragraphs?

- Does the essay address the reader directly as 'you'? If so, why?

- Does the first line of the introduction engage or 'hook' you—or does the writer just introduce the topic?

- Does the introduction develop by providing some context, or background information about the essay topic, or does the writer merely comment on the topic? Why do you think the introduction developed the way it did?

- Does the conclusion consider the implications of the essay's development?

- Does the conclusion provide the writer's evaluation of the topic?

- Does the essay provide a coherent, unified discussion of the topic?

CLASSIFICATION ESSAY

The Best Spectator Sports

As a child, my grandparents watched golf tournaments on the TV whenever they babysat my sisters and me. Apparently, they enjoyed watching other people golf. I did not. I preferred more exciting programs like Wonder Woman, who moved faster and accomplished more than the golfers on the TV. As I got older, however, I discovered several sports that I did enjoy watching as a spectator. Some of the more exciting spectator sports are team sports, individual contests and exhibition sports.

Team sports draw the most enthusiastic spectators. Thousands of fans paint their faces to attend professional football games, and nearly everyone watches the Super Bowl, even if their own team isn't playing. Soccer fans sport soccer jerseys and follow their teams with almost fanatical devotion. Soccer enthusiasts gather to watch the World Cup, which lasts for weeks. Finally, baseball fans attend dozens of games and calculate statistics for their favorite players. They may not paint their faces, but most cities throw a victory parade attended by thousands if their home team wins the World Series.

Races generate passionate support as well. Millions of people watch the Indy 500 and buy NASCAR jackets and other paraphernalia. Other people attend horse races, and some of them bet on the outcome, although some people just love watching the horses. Still another popular race involves different running events. The Boston Marathon and the Ironman Triathlon feature some of the most dedicated athletes in the world. They draw thousands of on-site spectators, although these races may be more exciting to watch on television, where the fastest athletes get full coverage.

A final category might be called exhibition sports. These sports feature individuals who have perfected a number of highly technical skills in a specific sport. Gymnasts, for instance, master difficult skills such as performing aerial flips and spins on a four-inch beam. Male gymnasts, on the other hand, demonstrate extraordinary strength on apparatuses such as the pommel horse and still rings. Similarly, figure skaters perform intricate footwork and difficult jumps while couples perform challenging lifts and throws. In exhibition sports like these, athletes combine strength and grace, making them especially satisfying to watch.

Almost everyone enjoys gathering with friends to watch a major sporting event on the TV. But while watching sports is fun, participating in active sports can be even more gratifying. Not only do participants contribute to the team effort and partake in team spirit, they get exercise and practice skills as well. In addition, people who watch and play sports make friends and often keep them. No wonder sports are America's favorite pastime. Sports offer something for everybody.

PROCESS ESSAY

How to Make Christmas Cookies

Every December, our family sets aside time for a very special holiday tradition: baking White Velvet Cutout Christmas Cookies. Making the cookies takes three days, but their velvety texture and sweet flavor warrant the effort. People often wonder what gives the cookies their unique flavor, and actually the cookies do have a secret ingredient: cream cheese. People often say that certain foods melt in their mouth, but our White Velvet Cutout Cookies really do. In this essay, I will describe how we make them.

On the first day, we make the dough. We prepare for this process in several ways. For instance, we remove butter and cream cheese from the refrigerator hours in advance so that they soften. We also double-check to make sure that we have all of the ingredients we'll need. The next step, mixing up the dough, requires an electric mixer. First, we cream the butter, cream cheese, and sugar; we add egg yolks and vanilla next. Finally, after sifting the dry ingredients together, we fold them into the creamed mixture before turning on the mixer at a low speed. When the dough forms, we shape it into a mound, put it on a sheet of plastic, wrap it tightly, and place it in the refrigerator to chill.

The next day, we preheat the oven before doing anything else. Then, we prepare the dough. After removing it from the plastic wrap, we divide the dough into three parts and store two of them back in the refrigerator until we need them. Then we sprinkle flour on the work surface and roll the dough to about ¼ inch thickness with a rolling pin. Making sure to dip the cookie cutters in flour, we choose our favorite shapes and press them into the dough. We carefully place the shapes on a cookie sheet. Once we have filled the sheet, we put it in the pre-heated oven and bake the cookies until just a touch of golden brown appears around the edges of the cookies. At that point, we remove the cookie sheet from the oven and transfer the cookies to a cooling rack. When the cookies cool, we store them in plastic containers.

Finally, we decorate the cookies. Before we can decorate, however, we need to make frosting. We put two tablespoons of butter and a cup of confectioner's sugar in the mixer and blend them until the mixture is crumbly; then, we add a tablespoon of milk and a splash of vanilla for flavor. Then, we keep adding confectioner's sugar until the frosting achieves an easy-to-spread consistency. Before frosting the cookies, we divide it into bowls and add red, green, and yellow food coloring. Because the frosting dries quickly, we also locate colored sugar, cinnamon drops, and decorating sprinkles so we can apply these immediately. Finally, we spread frosting on each cookie, adding decorative touches as we go. We set the completed cookies on a flat surface to dry.

All that remains is arranging the cookies on a plate and eating them. Waiting until the cookies are ready to eat is probably the most difficult part. Even though making White Velvet Cutout Cookies requires several days and lots of work, the effort is definitely worthwhile. Making cutout cookies is a wonderful family holiday tradition.

Definition Essay

What is a Friend?

Facebook has revolutionized friendship. Once upon a time, you had to actually know people to be friends with them. Now, people "friend" people they've never even met, so that it's not unusual for a person to have hundreds and even thousands of friends and still have no one to hang out with on a Saturday afternoon. This strikes me as very strange. In my opinion, a friend is more than someone who likes your comments. Sure, a friend might be someone who shares ideas and interests, but the best friends care enough to help one another grow.

Friendship at its most basic level can be defined as a relationship of two people who are not enemies. Some friendships are based on two people being on the same side of either a physical competition or an ideological issue. For instance, members of a softball team might consider themselves to be friends with other members because they spend time together and work for the same goals. Similarly, people who share ideas on political issues often behave like friends, chatting amicably and drawing one another out in conversation, even if they have never met before. Both types of friendships are very limited, however. Someone who shares a political view or who plays on the same soccer team is not necessarily someone who will also be willing to lend you money or give you a ride when you need one. Also, should you quit the team or change your mind about the viewpoint you had earlier, the friendship dies.

A more substantial friendship involves practical help. This kind of friend is willing to "be there" when you need help or just feel lonely. Although this kind of friend is much closer than the not-enemies kind of friend, the offer of help usually implies the expectation of help in return. For instance, one friend might be willing to help another with math homework, but unless the friend offers something in return, whether that something is help on an essay, amusement, social status, or just companionship, the person will probably not continue offering to help with math. Similarly, a person who wants to spend time with another person but is continually rejected will usually give up on the friendship because the other person isn't fulfilling his or her part of the bargain. Although most people consider the friends to whom they look for help and companionship their closest friends, these friendships are actually social contracts that can and often do get broken.

The best kind of friendship helps both people to grow. The best kind of friend will be generous, kind, honest, and honorable: such a friend offers help because it is in his or her nature to offer help, and such a friend says kind things because he or she truly sees the good in others. Of course, anyone would admire the good qualities of an individual like this and covet his or her good opinion, often striving in some way to earn it. For instance, if a person admires someone who values volunteerism, that person will probably find a way to volunteer in the community. Of course, with such a friendship, the same will be true for both friends: both will exhibit the best qualities and inspire the other to improve themselves. And while friends like these might also share ideas or interests, their friendship is stronger and less likely to die because it is founded on principles that never change.

Good friends teach us how to be and view friends. Once, a friend of mine told me about a childhood experience in which she told a girl that she considered her to be her best friend. The girl was flattered, but replied that she ranked my friend third or fourth best. Needless to say, my friend felt hurt, and she never bothered ranking people again. Instead, she decided to consider every friend someone to cherish. That is, perhaps, what baffles me about the idea of having hundreds of friends on Facebook: How can anyone cherish anything they have so much of? Can two hundred people all be friends? Two hundred of anything else would be called a collection. And while a collection of like-minded people may be occasionally convenient, I think most people yearn for real friendship. Friends are not to collect, but to cherish.

Literary Analysis/Classification Essay

Good and Evil

in *The Lord of the Rings*

J.R.R. Tolkien's epic trilogy *The Lord of the Rings* contrasts good and evil. As a fantasy, the books contain many fantastic characters such as wizards, elves, and dwarves. Some of these characters Tolkien consistently depicts as embodying good, while others continually do evil. Still other characters struggle with choosing between good and evil. In this essay, I will examine Tolkien's portrayal of good and evil through his characters.

A few characters in *The Lord of the Rings* always exemplify goodness. The elves, for instance, seem to represent purity and goodness. When elves first appear, the very sound of their singing wards off the Black Riders, who are seeking Frodo to capture the One Ring. Although Sauron's rings deceive and corrupt the greedy and power-seeking dwarves and men, the rings never affect the elves. Another example of a purely good character is Tom Bombadil. Like the elves, Frodo's ring has no power over him because he has no desire for power, wealth, or glory. Tom Bombadil's contentedness makes him a wise steward in his realm that even the willow trees willingly obey; because he does not demand obedience, his leadership never resembles tyranny.

Other character types Tolkien depicts negatively. The orcs, for instance, act selfishly and quarrel continually; they inflict violence and essentially exemplify viciousness in every possible way. When the orcs kidnap Merry and Pippin, the orcs fight about where to take them. When another group of orcs discover Frodo's mirthril vest, a deadly brawl breaks out over who will take the vest as booty. So hopelessly selfish are the orcs that the only way they can accomplish anything at all is when some evil overlord threatens them with violence. Another evil character is Shelob, the ancient spider who eats her victims alive. Like the orcs, Shelob is entirely selfish; unlike the orcs, her only ambition seems to be immortality. Content to live on whatever prey happens her way, Shelob's entire existence is one of robbing life to continue her own.

Most of the characters in *The Lord of the Rings*, however, Tolkien depicts more realistically. Of the dwarves, hobbits, wizards, and men, some fight for good and some for evil, but those who choose to fight for evil often do so because they have been deceived. Like most people, Tolkien's main characters face temptations and, wanting to do good, nevertheless struggle to choose well, rationalizing that perhaps good will result from doing wrong for the right reason. The best example of such a character is Boromir, a basically good man who uses his physical strength to rescue the hobbits on Mount Caradhras and bravely offers to fight the terrible Balrog with Aragorn, but who believes that the One Ring could help Gondor overthrow Sauron. Because he wrongly believes that he would be strong enough to resist its evil influence, Boromir eventually attempts to overpower Frodo and steal it, unaware that the ring's evil influence was already affecting him. But Tolkien does not let readers brand Boromir as evil in the end, as Boromir goes on to defend Merry and Pippin from orcs and even confesses his betrayal to Aragorn before he dies. His repentance makes readers realize that people are not evil, just because they make terrible mistakes.

I think that Tolkien wrote *The Lord of the Rings* with more complicated characters than simply good or evil characters because he understood people well. Most people want to be good, but many make bad decisions because they have been deceived or because they think they are strong enough to do the right thing when they're not. It is interesting that the best and most noble character Tolkien depicts in his trilogy is Aragorn, who resists the temptation to take the ring when Frodo offers it to him and who bravely faces horror and even death for the sake of others. And yet, even Aragorn has a bad day when all his choices go awry. Tolkien does not let his readers think that some people are good and others are evil, or even that by choosing well most of the time they can escape every bad consequence. Tolkien clearly believes that good and evil are real and that people can choose one over the other, but he also suggests that, although people may try to do what is best, everyone sometimes chooses wrong. Like Boromir, we all sometimes need forgiveness.

EXPLANATORY ESSAY

How the Europeans Conquered North America

When Europeans arrived in the 16th century, Native American tribes were thriving. The native people understood the seasons and the land; they practiced agriculture and hunted game to survive the harsh winters. Although the tribes sometimes argued, mainly tranquility prevailed between the different native peoples. In short, Native Americans flourished. When the first Europeans reached America, none of them had the skill or knowledge and few had the discipline or dedication to survive in the rugged land. The first colonies suffered devastating loss of life due to sheer ineptitude, and without the assistance of native peoples, more would have died. So why, when the Native American peoples had all of the advantages, did Europeans so quickly conquer them? The answer lies in three seemingly unrelated reasons: the Europeans had more advanced technology, took advantage of tribal rivalries, and spread diseases among the Native American peoples.

When Europeans arrived, the Native Americans immediately noticed their weapons. The Native Americans had not developed metal-working, and the shiny steel caught their eyes, as did the guns' loud discharge and powerful impact. When conflict broke out between the two groups, the guns intimidated the Americans, who believed the Europeans' guns superior to their own bows and arrows. In fact, the bows and arrows were faster and more accurate than guns were at that time, but the Native Americans did not realize this. Impressed by European technology, Native Americans soon abandoned their arrows and traded furs and food for European guns.

Native American tribes engaged in warfare among one another before the Europeans arrived, but generally they fought to recuperate resources or avenge wrongs, never to eradicate an entire people. The arrival of the Europeans changed all of that. The Europeans wanted possession of the land that Americans relied on for survival and thus refused to surrender. With their existence threatened, the Americans should have united in resistance, but the savvy Europeans forged strategic alliances to brew discord among them.

Divided, distracted, and distrustful of one another, the native peoples grew weaker, even as the Europeans gained a stronger foothold on the land. The infighting weakened the Americans, leaving them vulnerable to attack. By the time a few native leaders realized what was happening and called for all native peoples to unite, their numbers had already diminished, and their resistance proved futile.

The Europeans' most effective strategy for defeating the Native American peoples, however, was purely accidental: diseases such as smallpox, measles, and influenza decimated the native peoples, who had no immunity to the diseases, nor did native medicine men have antidotes or remedies. The viruses quickly overwhelmed the indigenous population, devastating some nations so much that they were wiped out entirely. As disease depressed the numbers of Native Americans and weakened their peoples, the growing number of European settlers grew stronger and more confident that Providence was on their side.

In fact, Providence had little to do with it. The Europeans gained control over American land mainly because as a people, they were shrewder, higher-tech, and just plain luckier than the Native Americans. Still, the Native peoples, whose skills and military prowess were actually superior, were initially gullible and distracted by the loud and shiny toys and the smooth talk of the Europeans. Seemingly innocuous, these small failings eventually caused the Native American nations' collapse, and Europeans ruled what once was no man's land.

Process Essay

How to Solve a Quadratic Equation

How do you solve a quadratic equation? The most expedient way is to check the answer in the back of the book. But that would be wrong, very wrong. Therefore, you should probably use one of the methods approved of by the math teaching community of the world. Approved methods for solving quadratic equations include factoring, completing the square, and using the quadratic formula.

The first way to solve a quadratic equation involves factoring. This method requires you to put the equation in standard form. Standard form is when you put all of the polynomials in the order of descending powers on one side of the equation and make the equation equal to zero. Next, you factor the equation. Sometimes, factoring an equation is easy. For instance, if you start with the equation, $x^2 + 4x + 4$, you can easily see that $(x + 2)$ times itself will result in that equation. Once you have factored the equation, simply decide what number would make the equation equal to zero. In this example, -2 would make $(x+2)$ equal zero. Thus, the solution to this equation would be -2.

If you can't solve a problem easily by factoring, you can try to solve it by completing the square. Start by writing the equation out so that the integer is on the other side of the equation. Assuming the monomial to the first degree is even, you should be able to figure out what number would make the equation the square of a binomial. Add that number to both sides of the equation. Then solving the equation is merely a matter of taking the square root of each side.

If neither of these methods work, you should use the quadratic formula. Conveniently, the quadratic formula works for almost any quadratic equation. Less conveniently, you have to memorize a formula and plug numbers in correctly to get it to work. Basically, you put your equation in standard form as described above. Then you plug your numbers into the quadratic formula and do the math. Because the formula involves the square root sign, the answer will include a square root, as in x equals 6 plus or minus the square root of 47, which for some reason is unsatisfying. Unfortunately, you can't do anything about that.

To double check your answer, you can plug the numbers back in to the original problem for both the factoring and the completing the square methods, but if you want to verify your answer with a problem that requires the use of the quadratic formula, the only way to verify your answer is to check the answer in the back of the book. If your algebra book does not tell you the answers, then you can just stop working as soon as you get the answer, even though odds are reasonably good that you messed up somewhere along the line.

PERSUASIVE ESSAY

The 4-1-1 on Phone Books

Every year, it happens. Phone books pile up in my mailbox. Once upon a time, only one came, but now two or three phone books appear. Some are white, some are yellow, and one of them appears to be "fun-sized." Too big to fit in a pocket, it's presumably meant to be popped in a purse or the glove compartment of a car. It's an innovative idea, but so far, I have never felt the need to haul one around, and my glove compartment has way too much junk in it to fit a phone book, even if it is small. No, the travel-sized phone book goes the same place as the other two when they arrive every year: in the recycling bin. Telephone companies should stop sending out phone books every year because most people don't want them, they waste natural resources, and practically no one uses them anyway.

Most people don't want to replace their phone books every year. Even people who still use phone books don't appreciate lugging new books in and old ones out on a regular basis. The majority of the information in a phone book doesn't change on a yearly basis, anyway. If a phone number does change, it's really not that big of a deal to cross out an obsolete number and pen in a new one. Most people would be happy to get a new phone book once every two, three, or even five years.

Replacing phone books with new ones every year wastes resources. An estimated five million tress are cut down each year to print the white pages alone, and only about a quarter of the people who get phone books recycle them. Even if some of the phone companies opt to use recycled paper when they print new books, they're still using a lot of ink and gas to transport the books. People who recycle unwanted phone books are still wasting resources, because it takes more gas to carry them to the recycling center. That's a lot of waste, especially when you multiply the number of households receiving phone books by the two or three books sent out each year.

On top of all of that, a lot of people don't even use phone books anymore. Many people use smartphones, which are cell phones with web-browsing technology built right in that allow people to immediately access the phone numbers they need via the Internet. Other people use the Internet at home to look up phone numbers rather than consult a phone book, which is more likely to become outdated. Finally, people always have the option of requesting a phone number through directory assistance by dialing 4-1-1 or accessing the service online.

Clearly, the time has come for telephone companies to stop the waste and the hassle of printing and distributing bulky phone books every year. If phone companies are savvy enough to realize that people are communicating with cell phones on the go, they can understand that those same people are savvy enough to use the Internet to figure out what number to call. The only reason telephone companies can possibly have for printing books every year is the profit they make on advertising. Businesses need to realize that people don't want to be deluged with phone books every year; phone book companies need to realize that two or three phone books a year is definitely the wrong number.

INFORMATIONAL ESSAY

Toothpaste:

You've Come a Long Way, Baby

In the song, "My Favorite Things" in *The Sound of Music,* Julie Andrews sings about items such as raindrops, cat whiskers, and brown paper packages as her favorite things. In my opinion, with the possible exception of warm woolen mittens, these are very impractical choices. What good is a cat whisker, I ask? I prefer things that I can put to good use. The automobile, refrigeration, Snuggies: these are practical inventions. But anyone who has ever experienced the agony of a bad toothache or the dread of the dentist's drill must include toothpaste as one of the best things going, especially when you consider how far tooth-preserving products have come over the last two thousand years.

Although toothaches are hardly new to mankind, toothpaste is. In the late 1800's, the first modern toothpastes appeared on the market for general consumption. At that time, the toothpaste consisted of a blend of hydrogen peroxide and baking soda which was packaged in collapsible tubes made of lead. Later, fluoride was added to some toothpastes, but the American Dental Association disapproved of the addition. Only after World War II did the benefits of fluoride for reducing tooth decay become widely accepted, but not until the 1970's did fluoride toothpaste become popular. Toothpaste advances since then have included cool dispensers, tartar control, and whitening properties.

Prior to toothpaste, many people relied on powders to clean their teeth. Abrasives such as pumice, salt, lead, chalk, crushed bones and oyster shells, and pulverized brick or charcoal were used to scour teeth clean. Unfortunately, some of these abrasives were toxic, and most of them corroded the enamel on teeth, hastening tooth decay. The upshot of these cleaners was that teeth looked and felt clean; the downside was that teeth quickly rotted and fell out.

One of the most interesting solutions for cleaning teeth in ancient times was the one adopted by many wealthy first century Roman citizens: human urine. Yes, that's right: Roman physicians recommended the use of urine as a refreshing mouthwash and teeth whitener. Especially prized was Portuguese urine, which was probably no different from regular old Roman urine except that the time it took to transport the stuff from Portugal had the effect of concentrating its chemical makeup. Ammonia molecules made urine a comparatively amazing tooth cleaning product. While effective in its own way, the Roman solution lacked the fresh, minty flavor most modern people prefer.

What an improvement a few thousand years can make! Quite apart from the sheer disgust factor, today's toothpastes reduce teeth decay far better than many of the remedies that improved the appearance of teeth temporarily but accelerated corrosion in the past. From Portuguese urine to the sparkle fun cavity protection of today, I think it's safe to say that modern toothpaste should be one of everyone's favorite things.

COMPARISON AND CONTRAST ESSAY

Prime Privies:

A Public Restroom Primer

Americans are spoiled when it comes to public restrooms. We are used to free and relatively sanitary restrooms in most public stopping spots. But when I lived in Ecuador, I discovered that clean and well-stocked public restrooms can't be taken for granted. In fact, over the two years that I lived abroad, my friends and I rated restroom facilities from one to five stars, and we decided that between these, the cleanliness, complimentary paraphernalia, and apparatus itself could hardly be compared.

The first point of contrast is sanitation. In Quito's and Guayaquil's most elegant restaurants, restrooms fairly sparkle. Upon entering, you notice the slightly sweet smell of roses, wafting lightly from a bouquet on an end table at the far end of the room. Marble vanities gleam and little pyramids of freshly laundered and rolled cotton towels rest near shiny silver spigots. The stalls, unstained by fingerprints or crude graffiti, stand proudly in the background. The toilet itself shines, as spotless as if it were brand new. The room truly merits its Spanish moniker: services, hygienic. In contrast, public restrooms in rural establishments in Ecuador are often filthy. After the stench, the first thing you notice in them is the floor, littered with paper towels that soak up whatever the wet stuff sticking to your feet might be. Next, you observe the sink, which appears never to have known Comet or Clorox or any other cleanser, for that matter. Finally, you cannot help but notice the toilet, which has clearly seen hard use, and recently, too. Like the sink, it is as much a stranger to the scrubbing bubble as to the cleaning wand.

The constitution of the apparatus itself varies as well. In five star facilities, the toilet has all of its parts. Lid, tank, bowl, float ball, flush lever—you name it, the toilet has it, properly installed and in working order. It even has running water. Alas, this is not the case with rural road-side stopping spots. In these, toilets rarely have all of their parts. Lids and toilet seats are rarities, although most toilets feature some kind of bowl. Due to the aforementioned sanitary issue, it's best not to actually touch the toilet itself if by any means you can avoid it. Flush levers, functioning float balls, and running water are also rare; however, a bucket of water is sometimes available if flushing should become necessary.

A final distinction lies in complimentary items. The five-star restroom abounds in these: toilet paper, soap, towels, and even water are readily available and abundant. Occasionally, a complimentary squirt of perfume will be offered by an attendant, whom you should tip if you accept the squirt. In contrast, one-star facilities offer few extras. Toilet paper may be offered for sale prior to entering or a roll may rest on its side on the floor, which if you remember, is covered in some mysterious wet substance. It is best to bring your own. Do not bother to look for soap; there is none. The only paper towels in evidence are on the floor or sticking to the bottom of your feet.

The two rooms are so different, they shouldn't share the name. Needless to say, the five-star facility is preferable. Use one any time you have the chance. If you find yourself in a hotel or restaurant that has one, you might even drink a little extra water, just to justify a bonus trip. On the other hand, if by any means you can avoid using a one-star public restroom, you really should. No sane person would ever choose to rest in one. The five-star facility epitomizes hygiene itself, but the one-star facility should be called 'Servicios No Muy Hygenicos.' That way, it would be clear. Between the one and five-star facility, there's really no comparison.

INFORMATIONAL ESSAY

Get the Message?

People communicate from the moment they are born: with their first gasp of air, they broadcast their first complaint. People communicate to make their thoughts known and to know the thoughts of others, though some with greater success than others. The people who are most successful communicators understand what barriers hinder the exchange of ideas between people in different situations. These different situations can be summarized in three models: linear, interactive, and transactional communication.

The first model of communication is linear. In this model, one person has a message that he or she communicates to an audience, who has the job of understanding, or decoding, what the sender means. For instance, a person giving a speech sends a message to the audience, and the audience tries to understand what the speaker means. If the speaker explains the message well, the audience will be able to decode it easily. Writers also encode messages for an audience. Whether spoken or written, with linear communication, the sender's challenge is guessing what objections, questions, or concerns the audience will have and answering them effectively.

Another model of communication is interactive. As with the linear model, interactive communication involves one person who sends a message and an audience who receives it. The main difference between the two models is that the interactive model adds feedback. Feedback is the sometimes subtle and often nonverbal communication that an audience sends to the main speaker. For instance, if the students in a classroom yawn or look around during a teacher's lecture, the teacher receives that feedback, understands that the students are bored, and hopefully revises the message so that it engages the students more. Other times, a teacher might ask the class questions in order to get feedback about how much the students are paying attention and learning, but whether the feedback is verbal or nonverbal, the teacher remains the person sending the main message.

A final model of communication is transactional. In a commercial transaction, a customer brings a wanted item to a cashier. The cashier takes the item, rings it up, and asks the customer for payment. After the customer pays the cashier, the cashier hands the item back to the customer. The transaction involves each person giving the other something and taking something from the other. The same is true in transactional communication, which is essentially a conversation between two or more people. Each person involved in the transaction sends and receives messages and feedback. For example, a person might tell a story to a friend, sending a message. The friend might receive the message but also glance at a watch, sending feedback to the first person that he is taking too long with the story. Receiving the feedback, the first person might then ask a question of the friend in order to engage him, effectively transferring the role of message-sender and adopting the role of message-receiver so that the transaction would continue.

People communicate most successfully when they understand how different situations affect their roles. Someone who doesn't monitor the feedback of others in an interactive situation may not succeed at communicating a message, while someone who doesn't interrupt a conversation to ask for clarification but only complains that the other person didn't make any sense will annoy the other person. Understanding the different expectations for communication in all three situations, therefore, can help most people connect more effectively.

Five-Paragraph Literary Analysis

Attitudes About Education

In A.A. Milne's short story, "In Which Rabbit Has a Busy Day," Rabbit sets out to discover the meaning of a mysterious note left by Christopher Robin. As he goes about questioning the other animals, it becomes clear that each of the animals has different experiences with and attitudes about education. In this essay, I will examine three of the attitudes seen in the Hundred Acre Wood.

Pooh, who has little experience with education, is humble. When Rabbit questions him, Pooh freely offers Rabbit what knowledge he has and apologizes when Rabbit discounts it as worthless. Although Pooh acknowledges that he isn't particularly smart, he delights in the poems and songs that occur to him without priding himself for his accomplishments, claiming rather that the lyrics just come to him. Pooh's humble attitude gives him a reputation as being a kind and friendly bear.

Owl, who others consider to be highly educated, is condescending. He tells Rabbit to go away because he is busy thinking, as if his thinking were so important that it should not be interrupted. Later, he feels irritated when Rabbit asks Owl about Christopher Robin's note and doesn't acknowledge that he can't read it. Instead, he waits until Rabbit gives him enough information to hazard an impressive-sounding guess as to its meaning. Even though Rabbit is actually more knowledgeable than Owl, Owl never lets on that he knows less than Rabbit. Owl's condescending attitude intimidates most of the other animals in the Hundred Acre Wood, and although they admire and accept him in their group, Owl has no close friends as a result.

Finally, Eeyore, who has learned the letter 'A', is proud of his education. He goads Piglet and lords it over him when Eeyore discovers that Piglet can't recognize the letter A. Later, when Rabbit not only recognizes but criticizes Eeyore's poorly constructed A, Eeyore stomps on the sticks, disgusted. Eeyore hoped that his knowledge would improve his standing among the other animals, but when he realizes that his knowledge is inferior to Rabbit's, Eeyore's puffed-up attitude deflates. Eeyore's pride makes him disagreeable to the other animals, yet Eeyore is pathetic enough to move the kinder animals to pity.

The attitudes of the animals in the Hundred Acre Wood realistically capture the way people feel about their different experiences with education. Some people delight in what they know and eagerly share it, careless of who gets the credit, like Pooh. Others seem to enjoy the high standing education gives them in the community so much that they don't seem to care whether their education makes them useful to others or not. Still others suffer as a result of improper pride, going from feelings of superiority to inferiority, depending on the situation. Of the three attitudes, Eeyore's is the saddest. I think most people would be happiest if they thought and acted more like Pooh.

The templates on the following pages can be photocopied and used to plan individual rubrics and essays, and paragraph progressions. However, you may find (as I have) that using a simple notebook works just as well for initial planning purposes. Although I may scribble out an initial rubric during a rubric-planning session with my students, I do transfer the information to a computer later so I can print out a neater copy.

The body paragraph planning template needs some explanation. You may notice the checklist of options in the left-hand column for everything but the first and last sentences. These options suggest to students what might come next in any given academic essay body paragraph, hopefully limiting the possibilities helpfully without overwhelming them.

Students who feel "stuck" can use this checklist to discover what the paragraph needs next. For instance, a student might write this topic sentence: "The Model T Ford automobile was not like modern cars." If the student isn't sure how to continue writing the paragraph, they may look at the checklist and ask which of the options might best answer the question a reader is most likely to have at that point. Would the reader want clarification, or a sentence clarifying how the Model T was not like a modern car? Would the reader look for an example of how the Model T was distinct? As you can probably tell, either of these might work well for this paragraph. On the other hand, a reader is probably not going to want to hear the student's reasoning about the topic, nor is there really a first step in a process to explain. So not every option will work for every paragraph, but often more than one will. What this checklist attempts to do is remind students what options they have to keep expanding upon their topics until they have thoroughly whatever point they're trying to make.

Individualized Rubric Template

Criteria	Requires Revision	Acceptable	Excellent

Essay Planning Template

Essay Type	
Academic Prompt	
Answer 1	
Answer 2	
Answer 3	
Thesis Statement	

Template for an Introduction Paragraph

Introduce the topic with a general statement or "hook"	Broad Topic
Provide a context or comment on the topic to lead readers to your specific focus	
State a thesis OR announce your intent to discuss the issue	Specific Focus

Template for a Conclusion Paragraph

Reiterate main points of the essay	Rephrase your main point
Discuss the implications or give your opinion about it	
Conclude with a final statement of some kind	Leave your reader moved, inspired, or impressed

Body Paragraph Template

Topic Sentence	
☐ Clarification ☐ Example ☐ Detail ☐ First Step or Event ☐ Reasoning	
☐ Clarification ☐ Example ☐ Detail ☐ Next Step or Event ☐ Reasoning	
☐ Clarification ☐ Example ☐ Detail ☐ Next Step or Event ☐ Reasoning	
☐ Clarification ☐ Example ☐ Detail ☐ Next Step or Event ☐ Reasoning	
☐ Clarification ☐ Example ☐ Detail ☐ Next Step or Event ☐ Reasoning	
Wrap-up	

About the Author

Dena Luchsinger is a homeschooling mom who tutors secondary and college writing students. Formerly a licensed minister, she founded Proyecto Down, a non-profit, holistic ministry serving families affected by Down syndrome in Monterrey, Mexico. Since completing a Master of Arts degree with a dual emphasis in writing and practical theology in 2009, she has tutored high school and college writing students, taught supplementary advanced and remedial English classes, and facilitated workshops for high school students and their parents within her local homeschool community. The parent of three children, one with the dual diagnoses of Down syndrome and autism, and another "twice exceptional," or gifted and talented yet learning disabled, she is passionate about students of all ability levels achieving their potential. In addition to her books published through Crecer Publications, Dena Luchsinger is the author of two children's books: *Sometimes Smart is Good/A Veces es Bueno Ser Inteligente* (Eerdman's, 2007) and *Playing by the Rules: A Story about Autism* (Woodbine House, 2007).

CPSIA information can be obtained
at www.ICGtesting.com
Printed in the USA
BVOW03s0425160517
484162BV00014B/150/P

9 780984 831326